Age of Restlessness

Early Life and Times of Robin Blessed - Part Three

Robin P. Blessed

PARTRIDGE

A Penguin Random House Company

ISBN: Hardcover   978-1-4828-9543-8
              Softcover   978-1-4828-9542-1
              Ebook   978-1-4828-9234-5

To order additional copies of this book, contact
Toll Free 800 101 2657 (Singapore)
Toll Free 1 800 81 7340 (Malaysia)
orders.singapore@partridgepublishing.com

www.partridgepublishing.com/singapore

CONTENTS

What Readers Say . . . About 'AGE OF DISCOVERY'

'Age of Discovery' is a cohesive yet progressive development to the preceding 'Age of Innocence', and draws attention to the events and experiences that shaped the author's life. Acknowledging God's footprint and blueprint in every aspect of his life, he illustrates how God looks at the people of the world. He brings to mind God's dealings with the two categories of people that make up the populace: The Wheat and The Chaff. An interesting and edifying read for sure.

—*S.M. Vijayaratnam*, Parent, Senior Manager.

Once again, Age of Discovery continues its thread faithfully from Age of Innocence, and serves out its purpose of revealing Christ through an unbeliever's life. It should help readers notice God's invisible but sure hand in their lives. It presents the case that while in vigorously attempting to deny God's existence, we very often end up 'kicking against the pricks' in unprofitable rebellion.

—*Cedric Tan*, Parent, Manager.

What Readers Say . . . About 'AGE OF INNOCENCE'

I have enjoyed your book tremendously. It had helped me to begin to appreciate the events in my own life. It is a book with deep and meaningful thoughts . . . a very unique book.

—*Wu Wanjin*, Educator.

God's hand is in all that happens and the book reminds us how His righteousness prevails. Robin is able to relay his story without hints of bitterness or anger, of haughtiness or pride. The writing style is direct, concise, clear, and relevant . . . without attempts to overdrive emotions yet with just the right precision to describe the intention . . . and space enough for those moments to hold back lumps in the throat.

The writing approach is uncommon in that Robin shows even as a 'natural' man he had yearned and search for his beginnings. Now, spiritually enlightened he is able to see that God was there all the time guiding the way . . . throughout his early life, and at the end it marvels me that the Lord Jesus stands glorified still in all the years that Robin had ignored Him. I hope for more of such biographies to become useful as tools to bring out the goodness of our Lord both to unbelievers and to fellow believers.

—*Cedric Tan*, Parent, Manager.

The book brought back many fond memories of my life at the age of innocence. Truly, "to everything there is a season, and a time to every purpose under the heaven". God makes each of us different and gives us just as varied experiences in life with people, incidents, and things around us; though we may not acknowledge God's existence then.

All things that happened in life, for good or bad, joyous or sorrowful, all were just transient and eventually came to pass and became part of our memory to be aware and by reflecting, to improve and consciously change what we can. Without awareness we are overwhelmed, drowned in self-pity and be unfruitful. Since knowing Christ, memories and reflection redirected my spirit to that of thanksgiving, of thankfulness, of gratitude to God for His longsuffering, goodness, grace and mercy upon even one lost soul such as me.

The author has likewise put together pieces of fond memories in his early life for a purpose: in praise and thanksgiving to the Creator, Saviour, and Lord in his life, and through sharing it that many may come to know this great love of God. *For all this I considered in my heart even to declare all this that the righteous, and the wise, and their works, are in the hand of God: no man knoweth either love or hatred by all that is before them.—* Ecclesiastes 9:1. May the glory and love of God shine upon the heart of every reader and be blessed.

　　　—*Samantha Quau*, Parent, Homemaker, Home-school Educator.

An interesting book to read . . . In its use of simple flashback in time, many fond nostalgic familiar glimpses of my own journey during the age of innocence came to the fore for reflection. Throughout, the book highlights the importance of acknowledging God and having a personal relationship with Him, who is the very centre of our lives.

　　　—*S.M. Vijayaratnam*, Parent, Senior Manager.

I enjoyed the Age of Innocence very much. I appreciate the author's reflections of his childhood—the past is not simply a distant collective memory of irreversible events, happenings and acts (and perhaps, omissions). A careful examination of childhood has shown the imprint of God's presence and provision. The past has its purpose, a purpose rooted in the source of the purpose who is the giver of life. I find myself reminded of a line in Shakespeare's *The Tempest*—"What's past is Prologue." Indeed, the past has, and will have, an undeniable role in the making of our current present and our future. God is the master weaver, and what an amazing tapestry we will see in the life of the author. This book faithfully reproduces the author's discovery of God's blessings throughout the earliest years of his life. Truly, God loads us with benefits, daily, from our beginning. Childhood can be full of richness. I am inspired. And I look forward to the Prologue that is to come.

—*April Mak*, Solicitor.

It is a book worthy of an afternoon curled up on the couch to look back in time: to reflect on what God and our parents have done for us, at the same time to count our many blessings.

—*Zhang Meifen*, Medical Practitioner.

DEDICATED TO ALL READERS

Readers are ALWAYS a special people. They are willing to set aside time to read the book they have chosen, and reading to know the author as a person who openly shares of his past—humanly deeds, innermost thoughts, and deepest feelings—as to a friend willing to understand the substance of his *written voice*. Wren and Bacon had come close in expressing my thoughts.

Choose an author as you choose a friend.
—Christopher Wren

Some books are to be tasted, others to be swallowed,
and some few to be chewed and digested.
—Francis Bacon.

A good book holds as in a vial, the purest efficacy and
instruction of the living intellect that bred it.
—Anonymous

The author prays this book and others in the 'Age of . . .' sequel, and perhaps more others that he may write, would be among the *some few* of which Bacon wrote about.

Perhaps, restlessness revealed dissatisfaction with the status quo in his life, in his heritage, in his environment, in his ideas, in his beliefs; they simply were unsolved problems. Yet all the hope in solutions outside of him was as much a paradox in that they were misplaced and provided no satisfactory resolution to the unsolved problems. Looking in to his questioning self or looking out to the wisdom of the world, he found no rest.

ABOUT THIS BOOK

No book is really worth reading, which does not either impart valuable knowledge,
or set before us some ideal of beauty, strength, or nobility of character.
—J. R. Miller

In this book, *Age of Restlessness*, the author shares his experiences and thoughts when he was seventeen until his twenty-first year. It was a time he reached out of adolescence, a time when he would be in his own man, a time that was a springboard to adulthood. Considerations during this period—about life, its purpose, meaning, and the things that must come to pass—lent content to this book. His two years in pre-university wraps up his time in formal education that was necessary to secure a place in university if he so decided on that route; another two and a half years in National Service was a compulsory mandatory draft into the Armed Forces. That all led up to his twenty-first birthday. Coming into that age was not of any meaningful significance other than having reached the age of manhood. The significance was in his *meeting with the Person of his life* then, even up until this very time of writing. From then on, life saw no variable in the sense that he found this person as an anchor who was also the foundation, the bedrock from which he would direct and live his life. There was only one sure constant, one clear vision, one sure purpose, with one definite mission that was certain about how he should conduct life. The world would challenge it in the changing circumstances of life, yet nothing would change because it was perfectly constant, an immoveable Rock, one that held fast and sure in some of the most fearsome raging storms and parched lonesome deserts in the author's life.

That person was Jesus Christ. It was the climax of the author's commencement in the new relationship with Jesus Christ, the Son of God; a friendship inconceivable for one who abhorred and avoided God, yet now as one who is joint heir with Jesus in the kingdom of heaven. Christ became his purpose in life. He was not just an ideal but was indeed real and perfect; someone he could always count on to show the way. The words of Christ in the New Testament that he read manifested without a doubt that He indeed was the Son of God came to us as man, lived among us as man, was crucified, and rose again the third day. He freed man from the bondage of sin that had shackled man into living dark lives from which he was unable to break loose. Christ was the only redeemer for him. Christ is the ultimate, the one and only. From then on, Christ was his all in all.

Life from innocence to discovery to restlessness stands out as though by design when the author looked back in time. Accentuated by a *staccato of events* in his memory in the *Age of Innocence*, followed by *little scenes* in the *Age of Discovery*, life now in the *Age of Restlessness* appears to him as clear passages or *stretches of time* in which events and scenes happened therein to fill the visible stretches of time. This age of restlessness was as a time trap, fixed in clock time. The author was unable to ratchet it up, or down; he was unable to do more, or less while trapped in the time and space defined or forced on him— two years at school, two and a half at National Service, and some months after to catch a breather. The five years was as though boxed-in, unchangeable from the outside, almost sacrosanct. Pa and Mie knew nothing about his two years of struggles at school and the extra accounting course that was pursued other than the results at the end of the year. No one knew of all that went about in the army camps he had moved to one after another, from basic military training (BMT) at 5SIR in Portsdown, to the School of Section Leaders (SSL) at the Singapore Armed Forces Training Institute (SAFTI), to the posting at 8SIR in Taman Jurong, and to 7SIR in Kranji. Pa had some knowledge of the high regularity with which he had extra guard duties at SAFTI on weekends; Pa watched, as his son seemed well with it. With Mie, the author had always given her comfort and assurance by making light of the experiences in camp. It was all very fast moving and National Service was almost as expected from those outside. He often wondered that National Service was as term-time service behind tall prison walls that no one outside really could know nor understand from where they stood on the outside, except for some who had been through it in a committed way. It was not about what you saw if they ever allowed you. It was about the times one went through, the experiences sometimes trying and ridiculous, oftentimes senseless yet offered much in learning—about so many things—of which the learning of human nature was invaluable. Decisions made were, in retrospect, often centred about the handling of people—seniors, peers, or subordinates.

National Service was a school of learning about human nature. It was a time that the character was tested, principles assaulted, purposes examined, and motivations revealed. It was a place where there was no need to hide from critical public eyes; there were none to look at as it was in its own world veiled from prying eyes. It was a time young boys-to-men herded into the same environment generally and treated alike yet imperfectly; it was a leveller of sorts. Few would think of standing out, many wished to pass through National Service—quietly and uneventfully without trouble from the handlers—basically to serve time. The common term we used was 'take cover' from standing out for good or for bad, to be lost in the mass until the time at National Service served out.

Life after knowing Jesus Christ became 'de-organised' to a new way of thinking and understanding not by force of a mandated structure or system. It was life regenerated from the very premise, the very seat of its existence to its conclusion on this tangible earth, it brought about a change, a transformation from the inside out. As a Buddhist, the author worked and laboured at doing good deeds in order to merit the good outcomes that would benefit his present, next or generations of future lives through the workings of a theorised unexplainable force of the invisible cause and effect of *karma*. How far that benefit passed on depended on the strength of the good deed. Try hard as he would he realised the limitation in man to attain perfection in truth; in himself similarly, the limitation was common with all and instantly ruled out the very hypothesis in Buddhism as untenable.

Knowing Jesus Christ did not require those deliberate workings and labouring. Good came from the inside out. When we have Christ in us, our mind and heart transform to conform to Christ's nature. Christ transforms us so that we become like Him. There was absolute liberty. Any goodness or a sense of right and wrong, better defined as righteousness where the right is without a self-centred motive, comes from Christ working His nature in us so that we think like Him, we conduct ourselves like Him, and become like Him. We cannot belabour or summon forth that which we do not possess. Goodness was not a property native to fallen man. Tainted with wickedness, envy, and strife at every act, man harbours an underlying self-centred motive. Every thought veils a self-serving end. There was nothing meritorious that man can bring to the court of God's judgement to present as worthy to appease the wrath of a righteous and holy God. God cannot excuse the waywardness of man; his wrongdoing cannot undo or redeem his own reprobate and corrupt nature. Man needs a saviour who can go to God to advocate for man, on the saviour's own account that has a perpetual eternal credit of acceptance with God such that in the Saviour's name, all the evidences for all the wrongs of this world be passed over when placed before the judgement bench. Man now can, on account of Jesus Christ, be acceptable before a Righteous God.

For man to save himself from his inherent and inbred wayward nature, the author had learned, was impossible. He therefore continues to miss the mark; he goes on to commit wrongs against God's ways. He is ever wayward headed for hopeless darkness. Only Christ as saviour can mediate between sinful man and an angry God; He only is able to save man for God will accept no other payment but the blood of Christ who hung upon the cross for all men in a *preternal* sense in time past and yet time future. God let His wrath on His only begotten Son who is righteous as the Father is. His Son was the only acceptable sacrifice to God upon whose head is the sin of all men placed.

The relationship with Jesus Christ was a very personal and private one. No one knew about it, not his brother Cai, definitely not Pa (dad), not Mie too for she would be too distraught and overly concerned. No, not even his atheist friends/classmates, not his Buddhist friends; not one soul, it was a truly well-kept secret. He did not plan to make an apology of his conversion or to seek approval from anyone for it; Christ was Supreme. He, however, required some time to think through when to break the news and how to do it. He could imagine the outcomes and the likely consequences, and braced himself for them.

. . . a time he reached out of adolescence, a time when he would be in his own man, a time that was a springboard to adulthood . . . Restlessness was a real matter in his life in an age of discontinuities in the social, economic, and geo-political milieu that nations once isolated by geography were beginning to manifest their influence over each other all over the globe.

INTRODUCTION

My heart leaps up when I behold a rainbow in the sky:
So was it when my life began; so is it now I am a man;
So be it when I shall grow old, or let me die!
The Child is father of the Man;
I could wish my days to be bound each to each by natural piety.
—William Wordsworth

Innocence speaks of, in the graver sense, an absence of guilt, the absence of pollution or contamination; we may usually think of childlike exuberance, an honest sense of wonderment, of childlike folly not necessarily foolish, just purely simple. The author's first book, *Age of Innocence* covered his life between age three and twelve. In his second book, *Age of Discovery* he shares his life between age thirteen and sixteen, a period of time when spontaneity took on a little more deliberation and his outlook became more intuitive, more considered, a little more preponderous. There was a heaviness added, a gravity new, that he cannot ignore. He learned more about happenings not just those in his immediate living but also about the world at large. Why do things come to pass the way they do elsewhere in the world? Why do nations, governments, and people behave the way they do? Are they not as he, a human being commonly connected and akin in more ways than one? His *discovery* was that the nations and governments were in reality organisations of people or in the final analysis, their behaviours represent the people leading and/or running them. He came into the maelstrom to which he could not fully comprehend why man is what he is instead of what he could be, and why man would want to dominate or oppress another of his own human kind. His *discovery* was that he became a little more like the world, pressed on all sides to conform to its norms and ways. The conditions in the world about him acted on him, moulded his life somewhat, and moderated his thinking. He was entangled and seemingly unable to loose himself from its hold.

In this book, *Age of Restlessness*, the author shares his experiences and thoughts when he was seventeen until his twenty-first year. It was a time he reached out of adolescence, a time when he would be in his own man, a time that was a springboard to adulthood. Considerations about life, its purpose and meaning, the things that must come to pass, such as two years in pre-university necessary to secure a place in university; another two and a half years in National Service a compulsory mandatory draft into the Armed Forces seemed as a prodigal waste to a national purpose of which he could make little sense. Still it was a *mandated* duty of every able-bodied male Singapore citizen when he came of age. The physical demands in military training—firstly as a new recruit, then as an instructor, followed by an eventual posting to a fully operational unit—was a necessary diversion to take his mind off all else that had occupied his affections in the matters of life, mainly religion and what was to become of his future. Infantry training had framed his outlook to one of physical force as though that was the grain of life, and subdued his bosom that once seethed with youthful agitations in the spirit. Seemingly accidental, almost halfway through National Service, he received a posting to the Third Brigade Band, the Armed Forces' only professional military band. The Band had decided to force a solution of filling its ranks with National Servicemen who had the school band experience to temporarily offer a 'stop-gap' measure to its own ageing professional cohort visibly dwindling in numbers due to mandatory retirement as well as its inability to recruit new professional blood. It was a sensible and opportunistic solution in that the Band would now have a section of permanently employed regular musicians supplemented by a continually refreshed cohort of National Service musicians with band experience obviating the need to train from scratch. The working environment and culture in the band was more 'country club' in nature as professional bands generally were when outside of practice hours, and offered him time to think about the issues of life that had been temporarily kept under the lid earlier on while consumed by the rough and tumble of infantry operations. His restlessness surfaced once again and the search for life meaning and truth continued unabated.

With all his interests, activities, and education, the central outstanding issue that never went away was religion. Born a Buddhist, grew up in the faith, believed in its tenets, lived through them, expected to carry the beliefs for the rest of his life, to faithfully perhaps dutifully pass them on as a family legacy. That 'religious faith' had lost its sheen, its fervour in the course of time as he questioned his beliefs in their fundamentals, in the elemental, and found arguments against them. His beliefs could not hold up to the incessant questions that sought assurances but instead answered with doubts; they seeped, they leaked, and revealed a want of coherence, integrity, and reality. Yet he persevered without serious enthusiasm, without any desire to profess and own his 'faith', just hanging on to it dutifully. There was a consistently growing sense of restlessness that had grown bolder and surer of his disillusionment with Buddhism. Such was the intensity that he diverted his attention to the mystics of Buddhism and elsewhere, to philosophy, to the supposed spiritual elements of the nether world. In all of that, no relief was in sight as the enigma continued to frustrate.

Perhaps, *restlessness* revealed dissatisfaction with the *status quo* in his life, in his heritage, in his environment, in his ideas, in his beliefs; they simply were unsolved problems. Yet all the hope in solutions outside of him was as much a paradox in that they were misplaced and provided no satisfactory resolution to the unsolved problems. Looking in to his questioning self or looking out to the wisdom of the world, he found no rest.

Restlessness was a real matter in his life in an age of discontinuities in the social, economic, and geo-political milieu that nations once isolated by geography were beginning to manifest their influence over each other all over the globe. The world was truly a network of nations inter-related with and interdependent of each other. Complexities had come on board to take problems to the next level. Just as at home country we have challenges of our own, in our own immediate backyard where issues kept simmering underground for historic years began to rise to the surface for contention. They do not go away readily or be brushed off, and ignored. The more we seemed to know, the more were we at a loss. The more knowledge we accumulated the more restless we become. The more we have the more vexations come upon us in dealing with them truthfully. Yet the author has seen the contented simple live fully at rest in their humble work, dwellings, and station.

His soul constantly sought rest in an anchor that would firmly settle all things concerning the ultimate purpose and meaning of life.

Rest speaks of a cessation of motion: it speaks of 'quiet'. Restlessness implies motion of spirit or of the apparent. Why are we restless? We have not yet come to rest. Rest in what? We might equate it to peace and quiet, to the rest from contention for needs, that which we *must have*; and for wants that we *would like to have* for comfort, sense of well-being, and contentment. Needs and wants as we speak of here can be of the *material* and of the *spiritual*. Lack of the former causes certain hunger, thirst, discomfort, insecurity, low esteem, social scorn; hence the search to remove them by satisfaction or prevention of recurrence. Lack of the latter vexes the spirit, torments the soul, and causes an unfulfilled state, a sense of incompleteness, of misalignment with a dream, a view; hence the search to explain and excuse them. He was restless as he had not been able to come to grasp with his beginning or his end. In short, the purpose of existence was not definitive primarily because his belief system in Buddhism did not and could not respond to the quandary of his existence with any amount of tested coherence. His soul constantly sought rest in an anchor that would firmly settle all things concerning the ultimate purpose and meaning of life. It was as a huge burden of time past, strapped to his back from birth, that he joyfully carried on in honour of tradition, and now becoming obviously meaningless—troubling his soul, vexing his spirit—to the point that as a Gordian knot clasped about him, someone must cut it loose, to permanently free and set him at liberty. It was not as Alexander the Great attempting to gain the world, by brute force could cut it loose; it had to come from within his own soul. It was not a thing that the world could give; it was the spirit within that could bring on the liberty. Even with that available mode, the author does not have the wherewithal to meaningfully translate the possibility into reality. The divine plan was for the Son of God to come to man as a substituted sacrifice to pacify God's judgement on man in his waywardness and forever free him from the bondage caused by his fallen nature through the conviction of the Spirit. That Spirit can do its work of applying God's righteousness when man accepts the divine plan of grace and mercy by believing in Jesus' efficacious work on the cross.

We need to come to rest in our spirit, one that can only rest in our Creator in His deity, in His purpose, in His love and mercy, for His pleasure. We would have arrived as in inertia wherein our own will rests in His greater Will. We then move as He wills, fully at rest in Him without a lack of knowledge. We need to know God, the character of God, His Person to rest in Him. That knowledge of God will draw us to Him, will cause us to live as it pleases Him, to wholly adore Him and move in His person, His will. God made us for Himself. We cannot rest or find rest until we return unto Him, when the vacuum in our heart for love, for belonging, for assurance, for meaning and purpose thoroughly filled with Him.

Believers enter into a spiritual rest in Christ; they have yet not come into the eternal rest, for we live still in a world of trouble through sin of the wickedness in men and the devil. Unbelievers rest only in their natural beings; they do not and cannot understand spiritual rest. We have an inheritance in heaven that which we have as a free gift of God through the righteousness of Christ, and the grace of God. The Spirit is the seal and earnest of it, in working us up in fitness for that inheritance . . . . *for you have not as yet come to the rest and to the inheritance that the LORD your God is giving you.*—Deuteronomy 12:9. *But not as the offence, so also is the free gift. For if through the offence of one many be dead, much more the grace of God, and the gift by grace, which is by one man, Jesus Christ, hath abounded unto many. And not as it was by one that sinned, so is the gift: for the judgment was by one to condemnation, but the free gift is of many offences unto justification. For if by one man's offence death reigned by one; much more they which receive abundance of grace and of the gift of righteousness shall reign in life by one, Jesus Christ.) Therefore as by the offence of one judgment came upon all men to condemnation; even so by the righteousness of one the free gift came upon all men unto justification of life. For as by one man's disobedience many were made sinners, so by the obedience of one shall many be made righteous.*—Romans 5:17-19.

For both he that sanctifieth and they who are sanctified are all of one: for which cause he is not ashamed to call them brethren . . . .—Hebrews 2:11

Age of Restlessness . . . The one major turnaround in his life happened towards the end of the age of discovery. It was an event of religious conversion, more than just a namesake change but one that left a deep imprint of God's purpose on his life, one that swept him to a new way of thinking, to a changed mind and heart.

HOW THIS BOOK IS ORGANISED

Age of Restlessness adopted the frame similar to that employed in *Age of Discovery* for the reason that restlessness followed discovery as the author saw no solution to all that was happening in his life other than to go along with them and adjust or moderate to adapt. In that continuum, there was no sharp break from where it came, from his experiences; just simply more accentuated and exposed. The period from the age of seventeen to twenty one was a time trap, the key events were fixed, alike for all boys to men; there was no escaping except in the mind. The one major turnaround in his life happened towards the end of the age of discovery. It was an event of religious conversion, more than just a namesake change but one that left a deep imprint of God's purpose on his life, one that swept him to a new way of thinking, to a changed mind and heart. That, the author will reveal in the *age of brooding*—the central idea in the next and final part in the sequel of the author's early times and life—how he lived out that conviction in his new found Christian faith. The way was fraught in conflict with family and the world; where conflicts take root, afflictions and vexations necessarily follow. Our flesh is constantly at war with the world and our spirit often restless. In matters of the world the law of the flesh rules, when in Christ the law of the Spirit takes precedence and subjugates the law of the flesh to ineffectiveness.

The author began with his two years in pre-university at RI in the only available pre-Medicine class. After four years in an all-boys environment at RI, he now met and interacted with girls in a co-ed environment, still at RI. Some adjustment was required quite knowingly or unknowingly in interactions with girls that he met for the first time and perhaps to last the two years in Pre-U. It was a time too when boys were biologically tuned to taking an interest in the opposite gender. Early into Pre-U 1, his study plan for becoming a doctor ended when his father openly made known the family's economic constraints and suggested a shorter route to earning a living as an accountant. What appeared as a feasible end goal to the giver of it, turned out to be a challenging nightmare to the carrier or deliverer of that mission, fraught with demands on limited time to complete school work, and to complete assignments in an external accounting program that required much self-learning and discovery. Attempting to straddle two vessels demanded far too much attention and effort, and that heavily penalised the soul and dissipated any little energy he had left to decisively take the battle.

Two and a half years in National Service took him from a new recruit in basic military training (BMT), to training as an infantry section leader (SSL), all in the company of fellow travellers of similar pre-university backgrounds. He followed up with the role as BMT instructor in training new enlistees entering National Service. A subsequent and final posting in the infantry was as section leader in an operational infantry regiment popularly known as the Hokkien (Fujian) regiment. The company of people in this unit were completely of the rougher grain from a gravelled social background with significantly lower or no education, where the fist, strength, and bravado were the law. They mostly spoke street Hokkien, a Chinese dialect, generally understood to be the loud hooligan, lawless type at the lower end of the social strata exposed to street gangs, gambling, and prostitution. He met them all: the gangsters, the gamblers, those who plied in the red light districts. He had two such gangs to deal with, rather manageable. All the early training in the harder life, the principled and exemplary walk of his parents, goodly Buddhist practices, and various exposures and encounters, bore on the manner in which he dealt with them effectively. He in fact enjoyed the challenges not of the physical sense for he was a truly physically fit person; it was the people interactions that helped his understanding of human nature. Life was about acting out one's deep beliefs and searched principles. That acting out required courage and serious conviction as the 'rubber hits the road'.

Just when he was getting used to enjoying the rugged life and all its passing 'nonsense', a mandate from the powers above took him out of the rough and moved him to an all familiar military band environment. Life was to become laissez-faire, musicians were quite unlike infantrymen, allowed more room for creativeness and with less rigidity, definitely sloppy by military standards. It took two weeks of sickly adjustment for the mind to compromise; to move from the rough to the slack that caused the body to revulse and revolt. What unfolded was a life of ease, laze, and boredom that did not help the body or the mind. Still, it was all for good intent in the hand of a foreseeing caring God who allowed events to flow as naturally yet constraining and/or restraining supernaturally to direct His good purpose to bear on them. God created man for His own pleasure.

Nearing the end of his National Service the author *nearly* found someone he had been looking for much of his life but never quite got near enough. Nevertheless, it was many months before his National Service ran out that the author re-visited and found that someone who was truly uncommon in the most common of places, always there and available. Yet the author had always ignored him, kept him at bay, and completely shut him out of his life, treated him as pariah, as taboo, as nonsense, as made up and institutionalised. Unbelievably this Person came to him in the pages of the *New Testament and Psalms* (that was what read on the cover of the little red book; he had no clue what those words meant then) as a living voice, revealing his Deity, manifesting his great wisdom in captivating the hearts of lost men, in drawing them unto him. The author was one such lost man, treasured and now found.

That person in the four gospels (according to St. Matthew, St. Mark, St. Luke, and St. John) with a singular message was Jesus Christ, who was fully man and God. Christ revealed in those pages of the gospels his Godly character and essential nature: of holiness and righteousness. God came to the author's heart and mind, the place that held all his affections, his interest, his hunger for truth—his soul—and softly touched it with the gentleness of a loving and patient Father, unforced, no heavy hand applied. God took the author from years of *restlessness* to a place of *rest* in his heart, to a place only God can give. God gave the light and led the way to His truth, to life. He was not out of reach. Jesus Christ had an unfathomed and unfathomable depth of beauty that drew the author's soul to Him. He was God with us. It was a nature that no man had or can ever have in the course of a human lifetime. The author had never met such a one.

Reflection is the means by which the author looks back in time and exposes his life from the time of innocence through discovery, and to that of restlessness to see the manifestation of a purposeful design, only our Creator and God can conceive. That which once used to contain a *staccato of events* in his memory in the *Age of Innocence* followed by *little scenes* in the *Age of Discovery*, now appear to him as clear passages or *stretches of time* filled therein visibly with events and scenes. Reflection IS NOT about digging into the *past* to analyse and explain what one now is *today*. The past is not deterministic of the *future*. Every moment we live draws us to or away from the truth. There is no psychology about it; it is a plain and simple fact. We are what we are, selfish in nature, ever wayward, missing the mark always, ever rebellious against God. There is no excuse for us. Until we acknowledge Him, we remain as man walking in darkness. History does not make the man; man makes history. God directs the forward history of man.

Reflection reminds us of the debt we owe to all that has gone behind us, our past, and in a real sense, all that has gone past has been in God's design. We are therefore indebted to His preserving care and love in directing our way whenever we reject Him and drift from His path; that we take not the insidious forked paths and stray from His Way; in guiding our feet that we fall not into the hidden pits of temptation. He places in our hands the opportunities for His work so that we may know His heart and be like Him; He lets us meet with all in the common way that in us they may see the grace and love of God so naturally merciful, and the warm embrace of His fellowship.

In reflection, we can begin to understand the sad condition of man fallen from grace and that God in His abundant mercies continues to cover us in His Grace in Christ Jesus. That we can comfortably leave behind, if not forget, the once unbearable pains, and inerasable scars marked by deep wounds that hurt to the marrow, knowing He has forgiven us for like sufferings we have inflicted on others, and to know He had allowed them all for His Divine purpose. In the same manner, we may see no reason not to detachably surrender all our glories, praises, and applauses from personal attainments in the world: for Jesus Christ, the Son of God gave up His heavenly kingdom to walk humbly as man among men. Despised of men in His lowliness, they derided and mocked at Him who, in willing obedience to the loving will of God, willingly hung on the cross as payment for our waywardness, so that in His invested willingness we may have the hope of reconciliation to God.

Where your treasure is there will your heart be also. In reflection, we may see that our treasure is in Christ; our treasure is our hope in Christ, no more and no less for in Him is all things. We must not take our eyes off Him, for we have no reason to turn to another.

PROLOGUE

My heart is inditing a good matter: I speak of the things which I have made
touching the king: my tongue is the pen of a ready writer.
—Psalms 45:1

And seekest thou great things for thyself?
Seek them not: for, behold, I will bring evil upon all flesh, saith the LORD:
but thy life will I give unto thee for a prey in all places whither thou goest.
—Jeremiah 45:5

At the outset, I will say that I have been highly conscious that my
experiences in the Age of Innocence, the Age of Discovery, and the
Age of Restlessness—the subject of this book—and in the next one
to come, the Age of Brooding, are those with which many of my
readers can identify. In the earlier two books and some of this book,
the content reeks of nostalgia in the background, and also definitely
of a certain kinship in our beliefs. What I have passed through you
have similarly experienced with varying degrees, and perhaps in your
reading you would begin to re-live your own experiences as you reflect
upon them as I often had. In the reflection, my prayer and hope is that
you can be grateful and thankful to your Creator for all His mercy and
grace. I am grateful to one of my readers who had very well reminded
us, when quoting from Shakespeare's *The Tempest* that "what's past is

Prologue," I likewise pray your past will reveal and manifest God's eternal Will for your short sojourn in this temporal space and time, as you move forward in life. May our yesterdays well reflected and shared, be as gossamer blown by the winds of tomorrow and scattered to fall on ready and willing hearts that see the goodness and mercy of our loving and gracious God.

The conceivable—two years at pre-university was a sort of bridge between secondary school education and tertiary university education. After pre-university there was a further two and a half years in National Service, a kind of mandatory military service to infuse a sense of national patriotism or preparation for war readiness, for which cause probably matters little now. One thing following the other, on reflection, turned out in a manner less than straightforward. Several situations reared their heads to cast the wrench in the works. *Firstly*, the plan to pursue medical studies ended abruptly and quickly at the start. That was a good thing to happen as it laid a clear cut resolution that no further consideration would be entertained. The matter was dead from the start, an idea that was still born. *Secondly*, the plan to parallel accounting studies with the pre-university course simply meant both balls had to be kept up in the air, not one must fall to the ground as a result of the laws of nature or a defiance of them. There was not one to choose. *Thirdly*, I had no intense interest in the subjects in pre-university except for General Paper—all about English and essays— that provided a wide space for the mind to roam. Keynesian theory in macroeconomics was a delightful diversion in introducing economic modelling in its most basic form. Biology and Chemistry was somewhat related to nature and made sense; I liked them but not with any great intensity of interest, not a fanatic to fervently pursue them. Physics was totally down a different lane and I had little wonderment for the subject. It was to have been a practical kind of subject that we had to largely imagine about instead, particularly in atomic physics. In the age of innocence, all was wonderment. Less wonderment, more of deliberate intuitive consideration dominated in the age of discovery. Now, in an age of restlessness, anything that does not yank up intense interest can expect certain disinterest from me and naturally die. I was truly undone and there was nothing I could do about it. With the way paved, what really could interest one, while straying could only prove detrimental? *Fourthly*, my perception of National Service was at its excited peak before I entered the Service and I wanted to be a commissioned officer. After entry, disillusionment enigmatically mocked at my aspiration, affected adversely by the things I saw in the early days in training; the standards of command and control and of leadership appeared as appalling. My dream of becoming an officer was not to be as the thought of it turned detestable; I could not accept the idea of becoming one that the wretched system defined. *Finally*, the good Lord planted the seed of yearning for Him in my heart paving the way for my conversion to take root; He changed my circumstances or space, uprooted me from the rough and tumble of infantry life, returned me to music and the band in a manner most inconceivable. This move of His created the time and space for me to pursue the truth, the way, and the light.

What begun as conceivable in the age of restlessness, went through all that made it inconceivable, and ended up eventually with the conception of my Christian faith. Once again, who could do that work and who could cause it to be but God in His Providence. He works differently. He made the lame to walk, the blind to see, the sick to be well, the dead to arise, the impossible possible, the conceivable inconceivable. He sees the uncommon in the common; He breaks not the bruised reed, quenches not the smoking flax. Ah! How gracious! One so rightfully high and mighty, in His own righteousness, and in His love and mercy, gave His only begotten Son who lowered himself to the place among men, without sin; obediently and blamelessly walked as man, faithfully and ignominiously became the sacrifice on the cross for the desperate wickedness of unworthy men who are undeserving by all accounts.

The aura of tradition, of buildings that highlighted it in the old RI, is now missing at Grange Road. RI had become somewhat like the world now merged into its environment; the once clear line between old and new is now blurred. The new RI was as newer in the new world; the old had lost its charm, its sheen is gone.

1.

A New Kind of Experience

I communed with mine own heart, saying, Lo, I am come to great estate . . .
—Ecclesiastes 1:16

For every one that useth milk is unskilful in the word of
righteousness: for he is a babe.
—Hebrews 5:13

At pre-university level academic education had notched up for the author: from learning the three R's (**R**eading, a**R**ithmetic, and w**R**iting) in primary school with lots of individual and group participation, to a deeper kind of learning that went beyond knowledge acquisition to an engagement that drew on the affections, inclinations, and experiences. It had now moved on to a critical review: to having a point of view, and to agitate one's concept of life through the works of others who came before. Education was about having a basic knowledge of the things these philosophers, scientists, discoverers, writers and poets thought or did in order that we consider them to develop our own views. Sifting and choosing was

1

more important than following, yet the fetters were all ever present to make choice burdensome. Views formed in the mind still have to go through the crucible test for reality in due time.

There was the oldest educational institution with a more than century old property and attendant facilities less than aligned with the changing demands of the then current and perhaps modern education environment. A move conceived years before had now come to fruition. The new facilities reminded me of the same old soul in a new body, as old wine in new leather 'bottle'. As all things old have been well or poorly used, and replaced by the new, and when it was time due for the new body or new leather bottle to be stretched, very soon newer bottles have to be found to contain newer soul, newer wine early in ferment. Today RI sits at Bishan; it left the Grange Road location more than a decade ago. RI is the secondary school and next to it is RJC (Raffles Junior College) the pre-university arm. The aura of tradition, of buildings that highlighted it in the old RI, is now missing at Grange Road. RI had become somewhat like the world now merged into its environment; the once clear line between old and new is now blurred. The new RI was as newer in the new world; the old had lost its charm, its sheen is gone. However, I seemed unable to raise any great sense of joy in the move. Perhaps I had spent too many years in the old, had an attachment to it, all too familiar with my favourite crooks and crannies. Its idiosyncrasies privy to myself, the Raffles 'ghost' that conjured an ever watchful presence, the banyan tree that stood the whims of time, the band room where mysterious sounds cast imagined ghastly apparitions, the neighbourhood, and all that I would miss all too soon. To remember the old, some bricks from the old RI were moved and plastered up on a miniature obscure commemorative 'cenotaph' of sorts. As was often in times past, a rock or large stone served as memorial of sorts to mark a spot on which a significant event or occurrence had come to pass. These were rather immoveable memorials that were a part of the natural landscape as it was or hewn out of a rock in that state.

Tradition means giving votes to the most obscure of all classes, our ancestors. It is the democracy of the dead. Tradition refuses to submit to that arrogant oligarchy who merely happen to be walking around.—G. K. Chesterton.

1.1 New Location, vicinity, and travelling

We were at the RI location bordered by Stamford Road, Beach Road, Bras Basah Road, and North Bridge Road up until about early March of 1972 when we moved to the new Grange Road location three months into pre-university one. The new buildings had four-storied classroom blocks, looked quite ordinary in design, lots of lines and uniformity. At first sight, it was rather ugly in that although the structure and design seemed highly organised and functional, they in fact stood out as monotonous, with no intention to consider the aesthetic; there was nothing outstanding or spectacular about them except for the modern facilities, and a supposedly grand clock tower with SEIKO marked at the corner of it. It was a rarity yet ordinary. It ran on quartz, a big deal then. This digital clock with an orangey light emitting display (LED) stood in the middle of the classrooms and office block that spanned the track and field in a sharp dip behind the block. It chimed out a simple tune of Do-So-La-Fa . . . Fa-La-Do-Fa to announce each hour. The clock kept good time, and kept students and teachers on time with their lessons and movements between classes. It reminded me of the ancient Chinese practice of striking a gong to announce time though less precisely than the modern digital clock.

The main entrance and exit for vehicles were along Grange Road, a dual carriage road affording access from both sides of the road.

3

The entrance was one end of the sloping horseshoe or inverted U and the exit the other end of the inverted U along the same Grange Road. One gate allowed vehicles entry by ascending a less than gentle sloping gradient that rolled with the natural contour of the terrain of a former hillock where the old Admiralty House once stood. The road headed up to a level at the top that served as car park and also as the assembly area for use in gathering the school during the morning flag raising ceremonies and on special occasions. From the other end of the assembly area, a narrow road ran down to the exit gate at the other end of the horseshoe or inverted U. On the other side of the property ran the short Irwell Bank Road from Zion Road and leading to Paterson Road towards Scotts Road and Orchard Road. No major roads fronted the other two sides that were adjacent to residences in the area. One other access to RI was from a small side road, Kay Poh Road that led in from the main River Valley Road on the backside of RI.

The buildings that housed classrooms on the upper floors, with the administration office and the principal's office on the ground floor stood on the left of the entrance road access. The central block behind the driveway and car park used as the assembly area held the school hall that contained the hall stage and floor space marked out to alternate as badminton courts and additional space allocated to table tennis tables. Gone were the wood floorings that were ubiquitous at the old RI; everything here at the new RI was concrete or concrete coated over with special surface. Gone were the old creaks of disapproval and boredom: into the times, it was as *terra firma* sound, sharp, and slick.

On the other side of the U were the science laboratories in a three storied block. The laboratories took the lower floors and classrooms the upper floors. Squash courts lined the far end of the block and they took up part of the second floor space due to their height. Built-in link ways at every level allowed sheltered movement between the three blocks lining the U. At the end of this block were the squash courts. RI was the first school to have squash courts. Behind the school hall block was the modern gymnasium. There was also a modern mini audio-visual theatre. There were all the trappings of modernity that I supposed suppressed any deep sense of nostalgia for the old. All these created an increased range of the extra-curricular sports and activities of interest that allowed students to tap into for their utility and enjoyment. On the ground floor of the science block was the students' common room, a sort of gathering point for students to relax and socialise during breaks, a place that was warm and cosy with open spaces that contrasted the tight-fitting sardine-can like classrooms we packed into daily. It had soft sofas, headphones for music, tables, and chairs to enable casual, small and short meetings. I seldom made it there for the lack of time, and with it the lack of familiarity with all its available amenities. Also after a while, the place had become 'clique-ish'.

The block of classrooms and the administration offices overlooked the nicely green rectangular school field (used for rugby, softball, and athletics) surrounded by crisp new looking red tartan tracks showing the full eight lanes from the sharp white markings on it. In bright sunlight the track was a beautiful sight, the sun lighted up the grass to a perfect light green, the tartan tracks a one-toned red, the pure white line markings cleanly straight, and everything so marvellously real and at the same time seemingly unreal. The grandstand and spectator terraces was as one continuous unit constructed like an outcrop from the basement of the classroom and administration block which accommodated the band room in the centre of the basement with door-less lecture theatres or theatrettes as we called them, on both sides of it.

A late photo of the main block of the old RI. The triangular capital of the building was the distinct feature in these Victorian styled structures. Notice also the field in the foreground, all patchy, grass gone, dry, and parched. On good days and sunny ones, they were firm to run on though not completely levelled. On wet and rainy days, the field was forlorn and lonely.

These theatrettes were Spartan. The 'walls' literally were just wood strips closely placed to allow a peep from the inside and outside of them. There were no true acoustic wall panels to absorb or bounce off the sounds, just air in between. The seats, more like fixed benches, shared the same theme of long wooden strips laid on metal frames that ran across the room in three sections of seating. The seats stepped up gradually so that the lecturer stood at the low end talking upwards to the students on terraced seating. The writing surfaces were simply long broad strips of wood panels wide enough to fit a little more than an A4 or foolscap writing pad, and ran parallel to match the seating arrangement.

Looking from the side of the building one could imagine the stepped drop from the school's main building level on the hillock to its basement and all the way down to the field. Tennis courts lie on the far end of the field and track lengthwise. Gone was the clay court at old RI, we now had two hard courts with high fencing to keep in straying balls. A swimming pool was then under construction along the length of the opposite side of the track.

Travelling to school, the new RI at Grange Road was simply pleasurable for me. I walked to school every morning from where I lived at Prince Charles Crescent almost parallel to the main Alexandra Road with a distance of four hundred metres between them. My walking route from home went against traffic along Prince Charles Crescent by a shortcut along rough tracks (not serviceable on a wet day) through to Jervois Road. Thereafter, it was on good tarred surfaces along River Valley Road turning through Kay Poh Road and up the naturally crafted steps along the side of RI's track and field, and up to the school's administration block. I saved on bus fares and cut back on bus wait/travel times. The daily trip usually took no more than fifteen minutes when at a leisurely pace. There were days when we woke up late; a brisk walk of ten minutes would take us to school on time. 'We' is used here as my brother Cai also went to RI. Cai was as a shadow for much of our school lives. I went to Jervois East and he came a year after. I went to RI, he came along a year after, and when I left RI for National Service, he left a year after to also enter National Service. We took different routes, he became an engineer and I an accountant. When we were younger, he went everywhere that I went, we were as inseparable; we ran together, played badminton against each other, kicked ball with the neighbourhood buddies. Cai was as an alter ego, the quieter between us, less of a risk taker, a wonderfully predictable and steady doer. We sort of balanced out with our different temperaments. When I was keen to risk a venture, he would throw caution to the wind.

1.2 Back to a Co-Ed Environment

We had students from other schools join us in Pre-U 1. One could easily make out from their uniforms the schools they came from. They would buy the RI uniform that comprised a top white blouse tucked into a green skirt, soon after they settled in. That was for girls. Boys wore all white: short-sleeved shirts and long pants. The girls were from Raffles Girls, Methodist Girls', Singapore Chinese Girls', Fairfield Methodist, Nanyang, Cedar Girls, Crescent Girls, St. Nicholas, St. Joseph's Convent, CHIJ, etc. These schools ran classes up to secondary four so their students had to choose to enter a school that offered Pre-U courses; at that time there was only one junior college, National Junior College that ran like Pre-University. Today junior colleges (JCs) are a common sight. There seemed to be significantly fewer boys than girls coming into RI. All RI boys who started out from secondary one had been on the outside of a co-ed environment for four years of secondary education and those who stayed on, a significant cohort, were now re-entering a co-ed mode or rather we now have girls coming into or invading our all boys environment.

1.3 Physical size and the buildings

The Grange Road campus looked massive with the four-storied classroom blocks when one think of the typical two-storied blocks at the old RI. If one counted the basement lecture theatres, we actually had a hidden submerged storey. Yet the old architecture of the old RI looked massive mainly because of the high ceilings pushing up the height overall, along with the old system of large columns that revealed the huge cornerstones in place; it also had very large barren open spaces. The new premises at Grange Road looked modern and cleanly organised, having a neat design and with clear architectural lines in tandem with the times. It was simply significantly more functional and creative in space planning. One could sense when moving around the property that the public facilities such as the gymnasium, the track and field, the sports complex, and theatrettes, all exuded a sense of generosity in space. However, when one entered the classrooms, the space allowance was less kind and tended to eke out every inch of personal space for common use.

1.4 Extra-curricular activities (ECA)

There was little that had changed in the area of ECA except that with newer and better facilities the expectation of exceeding previous performances was high. The new tartan tracks expected seconds shaved off from all run times; one could feel a caressing spring when stepping on its surface. Squash courts were supposed to spearhead our pioneering efforts in the sport and aid training the wrist flick in badminton. The better field and scrum training equipment expectedly raised our competitiveness in rugby. We had a swimming pool of our own and that should bring on a new swimming era at RI. We even had a rather professional looking cheerleading squad of 'pom pom' girls and boys in the American tradition that did synchronised sharp movements, formations, and stunts. Callisthenics appeared on the scene as well to add to the pomp and circumstance.

1.5 Style of education

Progressively, the education at RI continued to spell of greater independence in approach, learners took up *responsibility* of their roles working their way in and around the system and *accountability* for all that transpired thereafter including work outputs and outcomes. There were classes to go to, laboratories for practicum, extra-curricular activities to work through, homework to respond to, assignments to support the lessons attended, standalone presentations to make, extras to volunteer in, and social activities to which one moved about and around. There was a hive of activities that kept school life throbbing, yet one does not have to be in all of them. I continued as before, with school work and the band my primary occupations. I had no developed abilities in the prior four years to break into any sports at school level, just only inter-class and inter-unit (uniformed groups) level sports such as basketball, volleyball, and track and field. Visits to the school library became more frequent than before as there was much to discover; it was no longer general knowledge; serious and new subjects became the draw. There was much to explore, constrained only by time.

1.6 Courses/subjects of study

We had five subjects to study: General Paper, Economics, Biology, Chemistry, and Physics. Mathematics, the ubiquitous subject had disappeared from our plates seemingly. It, however, made appearances in the Physics course in energy/ mechanics calculations and so on.

General Paper was as English Language at secondary level but containing a great deal more content, in reasoning, articulation of thoughts and ideas, and less of grammar, structure and the like. In a sense, it was more interesting. The teacher informed early on that she frowned unkindly upon grammatical and language errors. Three such errors immediately resulted in a failed paper. At pre-university level, there was a definite expectation that all the ten years of schooling at primary and secondary levels had provided a sound basis in the proficient use of the English language in articulating one's thoughts and communicating them most effectively. So, as the argument went, how can ten years of schooling and immersion in the language result in structural, grammatical, and usage errors? Three such errors deserved a 'fail' mark for the paper for it to be set aside as unworthy for further evaluation. The emphasis was with good reason, unquestionably clear.

Expectations may be frustrated but hopes are never dashed. As the author had learned from his years of growing up that when one door shuts out, there would nearly always be another door opened. It was a bit like a 'second life' to everything considered terminal or broken or a castaway, as not breaking a bruised reed, or not quenching the smoking flax.

2.

Expectations

U nlike the four years earlier, the author had no more greater *expectation* of himself other than to work through these two years in pre-university and to move on to university. It was as though these two years would wrap up his years of receiving and completing the right level of formal schooling to prepare him for a vocation that would very likely last his lifetime as a career. This was normal, as though formal education was the foundation of his life to which the pile had firmly laid. Changing course literally meant uprooting and laying a new foundation in another discipline that time and resources could ill afford. One could see it as the point of no return pushed from a tributary into the main stream of a professional career and eventually into the river of definite specialisation. By this time, one would have made up the mind on the course of study to pursue. It was again as that the tide and time waited for no man. The goal of education seemingly presented itself as one of preparation for a living, a living embroiled in earning a fitting income to commensurate one's education, the work for which one took up, to save, and prepare to raise a family, and wherever possible, leave a heritage, a legacy of sort. One's pleasure was in meeting these expectations of the age and times. The society expected it of him, his parents, and relatives as well; he came to expect it of himself almost unknowingly. Yet the restlessness simmering in him set expectations on the edge, taunting rebellion in the crack lines that showed up between the status quo and reality.

The author had clearly made up his mind to embark on a career in medicine, whether he was motivated by his sister Zhu's death almost a year and a half before, or by any serious notion of a respected profession as was common in those days to mean an accountant, a banker, an engineer, a lawyer, or a medical doctor. The former motivation was real at the spur of the moment while the latter had never really ever occurred to him even though he had a love for the law profession as he had watched it on television and felt a love for it. In a case as this, he seriously had no point of view but to let the first intention to proceed in the two years in pre-university and take up the medical course in university with a disruption to National Service. There was a demand for doctors and medical students could automatically defer their National Service; another reason was the longer course over other disciplines along with the required time to intern as houseman at hospital for the practicum. The whole matter appeared as simple as clockwork. This was very soon to turn out otherwise.

Expectation is looking forward toward something that will probably happen or come to pass, whether in hope or in dread. It is quite unlike waiting for a sure thing. Expectations hence may be frustrated but hopes are never dashed. As the author had learned from his years of growing up that when one door shuts out, there would nearly always be another door opened. It was a bit like a 'second life' to everything considered terminal or broken or a castaway, as *not breaking a bruised reed, or not quenching the smoking flax*. This was a philosophy that Pa had always practised and as son, he had come to embrace it well. A few months into pre-university one, Pa made it clear that the author had to abandon the medical course in place of accountancy, and there was not such a course studied at that pre-university level at RI. The alternative would come by way of an accountancy correspondence course from the United Kingdom. With little guidance or sound advice, that was the path he took. Practicality dominated the decision, there was nothing to like or dislike, and there was not a choice. It seemed as though that was the way life cut out to be. There were times in the past when we got to choose some things; while at other times, choice could not permit. Here was a case when life was as a joke, a teasing, and a quite unfriendly taunt. He wished it was not so but it was. Acceptance of the fact and working with the circumstances to make the best of them was the meek and lowly manner to proceed.

Expectations can surprise when disappointments unexpectedly turn up at the door. So he looked for another door to open. This door was opened by Pa—a quick swing door—that opened to something he knew nothing of, something he never could have dreamed of, not something he had thought highly of, but rather a profession that his uncle was into, one he never thought too well of. Could a third door open out of this second door? What's behind that second door one must first sort out before even thinking of the third. Come what may, there is always another opportunity ahead.

However, the studies opened my eyes and mind to the workings of the world, to the people about me, the events some of which characteristic of the times and others shocking, all bore impressionably on me. They were provocative and agitated my worldview somewhat, caused restlessness from time to time, agglomerated naturally, and congealed in time to cast postures in my understanding and appreciation of things about me.

3.

At Seventeen—Clear yet Hazy

For if the trumpet give an uncertain sound,
who shall prepare himself to the battle?
—1 Corinthians 14:8

The first half year in pre-university was about sizing the course entered into, how much to put into it to expect that which should roll out. It was a sort of settling in, focusing on the essentials of study, and adjusting as his socio-cultural life slightly altered from an all-boy to a co-ed environment. The subjects were different, of wider berth and deeper insight; the learning approach visibly independent and exploratory; teachers specialised in their subjects exhibiting sound knowledge as well as complete familiarity with examination requirements. We were there to prepare for further education and to make the grade. Education and examinations were as inseparable twins, since we entered school and now still.

We studied subjects to prepare for a medical career without a clear knowledge of the profession of a doctor, or engineering with little sense of what an engineer does or what a chemist does. What we knew about the discipline was all a generality drawn from articles or from the clinics we went to or a jaunt to Pa's workplace. A career expectation was a general *expectation* drawn from the general *perceptions* offered by influential voices in our lives that came from family, friends, teachers, and society. They, as you might have surmised, received their perceptions and expectations from those who came before them. However, the studies opened my eyes and mind to the workings of the world, to the people about me, the events some of which characteristic of the times and others shocking, all bore impressionably on me. They were provocative and agitated my worldview somewhat, caused restlessness from time to time, agglomerated naturally, and congealed in time to cast postures in my understanding and appreciation of things about me.

3.1 Girls . . . Prom . . . PM's Daughter

When we started out in the first year, the pre-university ones underwent a rowdy sort of initiation. There was to be a prom where everyone comes in their best party outfits and party in the evening on the school premises. One of the things we had to do was have a card filled out with the names and signatures of the seniors, that is, those in pre-university two who had been through this exercise the year earlier. Just as it was with everyone else, my card went everywhere with me to collect as many names as it could gather. I walked into a pre-university two class where the din was deafening as the boisterous students chattered and laughed without restraint. In the old RI buildings still, yet to move to the Grange Road site shortly after, with the high ceilings and poor acoustics, the cacophony was loudly cantankerous. In the midst of all the casual activities, there was this girl a little stocky with short straight hair who reminded me of my second sister, Zhu. She was at her two feet by two feet square desk, poring over a frightfully and mightily thick book totally engrossed in her reading. What a scene—stillness in a storm or a marketplace—she was as though oblivious to all about her, locked into her own world. I recognised her; she was none other than Wei Ling, our then Prime Minister's daughter. Related to a public figure, she was by default, a public figure. I walked up to her and asked for her signature. She did not look up, took the card from me, and simply signed the Chinese character of 'Ling' for her name. She pushed the card back to me, I took it up, thanked her, and walked off. That scene will always stick in my mind. In that few short moments, I caught an enduring glimpse of discipline, of an attitude honed by years of habit and training. Much I could write about it from the position of conjecture, reasoned and reasonable conjecture. Perhaps that is a subject worthy of exploration.

3.2 Switch to Accounting: Meet Jack Benny

After three months into Pre-U 1 Pa had a discussion about having me switch out of Medicine as he was unable to support such an endeavour. All it meant was for me to continue my two years in the same course and complete the GCE 'A' (Advanced Level examinations with no hope of going to university. It then dawned on me that it was reality and there was little any of us could do about. I fully accepted the decision and my immediate response was, "Pa, what would you have me do?" Pa seemed prepared for this and said I could go on to Accounting just like his oldest brother. The income was good and his brother was not even a qualified accountant, he had a diploma from the London Chamber of Commerce and a Pitman's diploma.

Pa tasked me to search the newspapers and see what I could gather. I found there were such correspondence programs advertised in the newspapers. I cut out coupons in the advertisements, filled them out, and sent them to several organisations in the United Kingdom to solicit more information. In weeks, I started to receive mails from them about their history, their value in the job market or within the profession. I considered the various relevant Associations and Societies (Association of Certified & Commercial Accountants, Society of Company & Commercial Accountants, Institute of Cost & Management Accountants, Association of International Accountants, and Institute of Chartered Secretaries & Administrators), discussed with Pa, further discussed with his oldest brother on the weekend. My uncle did little to offer by way of advice. I therefore chose one (SCCA) among four major ones to register my membership. Years later, I added the ICSA after I received my SCCA certification. My application went out to the U.K. In a few weeks, RI received a letter from the U.K. asking the school Principal to endorse the application as a referee before the SCCA would process my application for student membership. He refused and informed my Form teacher who spoke to me about it. I explained to her how clearly important the Principal's support was as my family had made up its mind about the accounting route of study. She spoke to the Principal, Mr. Philip Liau, again. The Principal ordered that I went to see him. The next day, I found him along one of the ground floor corridors on his morning rounds. With some trepidation, I went up to him, greeted him, and announced who I was. He knew of the case, and without allowing me to proceed further, showed a stern unflinching face and demanded that my duty as a student at RI was to concentrate and focus on my pre-university studies. I was not to do anything else and that was the end of the matter. He clearly would not entertain anything else. I thanked him and walked away not really disappointed, in fact I was in agreement with him. Mr. Liau showed his mettle, well-principled man who clearly stood by his vision of what a student's role was, and of his own role as principal in charge of them. Every single student was under his watch.

Yet as bearer of this endeavour of switching to accounting, I had one more consideration—that of my family—with which Mr. Liau did not have to reckon. I thought that was the end of studying accountancy under Mr. Liau's watch.

Within a few weeks, I received an airmail letter from the U.K. informing of acceptance of my application with all the necessary information on getting started. There was some excitement in this additional endeavour. I did not ever know whether Mr. Liau ultimately acted as referee and endorsed the application and if he did, was my Form teacher instrumental in making it happen. My Form teacher empathised in my cause and was sympathetic to my request. It was not important to know the details. One thing I now surely know was that our Creator's hand was in it. The accounting route set, and the financial role cast, nothing would change it. Some years later, I became a regional finance and accounting director at a U. S. multinational company, and a rather successful one. Still I had never thought too much about accounting, it was essentially an important discipline to keep a business running smoothly through financial prudence among other things. As I moved up the business career ladder, I provided oversight and hired accounting managers to manage the day to day operations. Diligence, ability, skills, enthusiasm, willingness, and delight took me through many new roles in disciplines as varied as administration, human resource management, information technology, project planning, business modelling/systems thinking, customer services, marketing, strategy, business development, and productivity management. Accounting was the pivotal discipline that provided the lynch pin in the world of understanding and perceiving business. A business must make money. A business must also have business coming to it. Managing people—employees as well as customers— and their expectations made business work

By the way, Mr. Liau was the last principal from the traditional school master mould, a disciplinarian without the rod but his presence sent some shudders down our spines. He was tall and ramrod straight, not exactly lanky, walked his rounds with his hands behind his back in slow deliberate steps, no sense of hurry, never donning a smile, ever so stern looking. He had a shining forehead and a receding hairline, sparse dark black hair sweeping back, very smooth and fair-skinned, bespectacled in black rims. We all nicknamed him 'Jack Benny' after the American stand-up comedian by that name. He was a repellent: spying him from the distance coming our way, we would turn the corner to avoid him. Failing to find a feasible escape we would walk right on and reverently greeted him, "Good morning, sir," for the younger ones or for us it was "Good morning, Mr. Liau." He never returned the greeting but would acknowledge with a gentle nod. Still, Mr Liau was an exemplary head of the school, watching over his flock—teachers and students—and the facilities, curriculum, standards, and performance both within and without. He was a man ready to further the school's vision having been a teacher and then of many years at RI, totally familiar with its history, culture, and workings. Years before, early in his tenure as principal he was engaged in the plans to build the new RI at Grange Road. Simply, he delighted in his role, was diligent in his duties, and vigilant against all sloppiness/ backsliding. That made for greatness. I learnt from him simplicity in the execution of his duties, driven unquestionably from an unmistakable vision as a master educator; his demeanour left no doubt about himself, what he stood for, and how far he would go to stretch us to be the best.

3.3 Continued Interest in all that's happening

The news had always had a fascination for me. They kept my mind constantly on the go, thinking about the issues that highlighted the days and weeks and months ahead. At that time our engagements were real and our affections sincere; our agitations roused to meet them head on. For me they never walked into oblivion, they mellowed in time from the lack of relevance. The political, economic, and social settings were all very quick moving; nothing seems lethargic and if it was, it went on the wayside. All things were literally on the fly and our very thoughts and lives went along with the tide. There was no stopping it. Interestingly we were all still merely active observers—hearts and minds keenly tuned in to the happenings—and yet we were passive activists without the concurrence of experienced reality. We were in a state of 'virtual reality' to borrow from the jargon of our time. This was all very understandable with our lack of experience and having rather focused schooling activities to occupy us.

Time, the ever scarce resource, decided the extent of their impact on our lives; youthfulness set the bounds for what we can or cannot sensibly do. Life was very much that and very much for all that would come to pass—limited time, restricted by knowledge both cognitive and experiential, and skills—and by the time we have the knowledge and skills to continue the march forward, TIME imposes its ceaseless hold until we cease to live. Life runs in seeming cycles. Continued interest in all that's happening will one day fade as knowledge and skills, let's call it the 'heart', seek change—of affections, of engagements—and perhaps more accurately, it seeks the truth. TRUTH is Changeless.

3.4 General Paper

General Paper was as English Language at secondary level but containing a great deal more content, in reasoning, articulation of thoughts and ideas, and less of grammar, structure and the like. In a sense, it was more interesting. The teacher informed early on that she frowned unkindly upon grammatical and language errors. Three such errors immediately resulted in a failed paper for it revealed an inability to handle and deal with the English language. I supposed the argument was that one required a sound command of the language to convey ideas, thoughts, and arguments. The English language was the means of conveyance, or the *vehicle* of thought.

One book the teacher recommended for reading early in the course was *Straight and Crooked Thinking* by Robert Thouless. It was a book about the flaws in reasoning and argument. According to Thouless, *". . . cold, unemotional thinking is needed . . . whenever we have to make up our minds about a disputed question of fact. That I find fault with the use of emotional thinking in connection with such problems as tariffs, prohibition, social ownership, and war does not mean that there is no place for the emotional use of language. Poetry, romantic prose, and emotional oratory are all of inestimable value, but their place is not where responsible decisions must be made. The common (almost universal) use of emotional words in political thinking is as much out of place as would be a chemical or statistical formula in the middle of a poem . . . . Into the action which follows decision, we can put all the emotion which we have refused to allow in our thinking. Let us think calmly and factually about such evils as poverty, oppression, exploitation, and war, and then, when we have decided rationally that they are great evils, oppose them with all the passion of which we are capable.*

The growth of the exact thinking of modern science has been very largely a process of getting rid of all terms suggesting emotional attitudes and using only those which unemotionally indicate objective facts. It was not always so."

The emotional, which I had earlier termed as affections and agitations skew objectivity. Reason becomes clouded when tainted with emotional attitudes and simply becomes crooked thinking. I often wondered about Thouless' work and those I read about 'hidden persuaders' and populism that will be raised further down in this chapter, how they surfaced simultaneously in the age of restlessness where young excitable passions and raw nervous agitations provoked our impressionable immature thinking, and carried our visibly manufactured outlook. Was Thouless thinking about objectivity as associated with exact thinking in modern science as cold, unemotional and rational, and about subjectivity as associated with the emotionally affected thinking? The former objective thinking was necessary for making decisions while the latter emotional thinking was useful for acting out the decisions humanly.

3.5 Economics, Biology, Chemistry, and Physics

Five subjects—General Paper, Economics and three other subjects—became very much the content of our pre-university stint. Economics cut across all the streams—medicine, pure science, engineering, and the arts—and stood out as with General Paper, highlighting their primary places in our studies. Medicine had three science subjects in biology, chemistry, and physics; Pure Science replaced biology for mathematics; Engineering kept physics and added double mathematics (maths, and further maths); the arts had history, literature, and general mathematics. I had often wished I could swap physics for mathematics, quite impossible then.

Economics analyses the production, distribution, and consumption of goods and services. One of the early terms we learnt in economics was the ubiquitous *ceteris paribus,* Latin for all other things being equal and held constant, more commonly 'all other things being equal'. It was a pre-emptive statement to avoid unexpected outcomes, I surmised. Microeconomics was like looking at the 'micro', the details about allocation of scarce resources as land, materials, capital, and role of entrepreneurship in optimising the acquisition/ supply of these and the demand of customers. It focused on firms and businesses, households, and individual buyers and sellers.

One name I remembered quite distinctly was that of Thomas Robert Malthus because his theory initially sounded worrisome to me. Of course, it was after all only a theory. The premise of his theory was:

- Population, when unchecked, increases in a geometrical ratio.
- Subsistence increases only in an arithmetical ratio.

The contrasting increases in one of a more predictable manner and another in more exponential manner identified a potential 'astronomical' (just to dramatise its effect) disconnection between supply and demand. That meant that the means of subsistence or food production would not be able to provide enough for unchecked population growth. His theory was that population growth would of necessity be checked by the limited means of subsistence. Population will invariably increase when the means of subsistence increase. Throughout history, Malthus noted that societies experienced famines, plaques, wars, and natural disasters to mask populations overstretching their resources. Population, he concluded was repressed or levelled through such natural and man-made misery and/or vice. The repression was through natural means, and it frightened me then to think of the man-made means, literally human engineering. In my lifetime, I had seen it attempted at home base and was grateful the error soon discovered, was de-engineered. Man must not play God; the repercussions are far-reaching, painful, and deleterious. The short-term view or theory thought to benefit the times when in hindsight often revealed its irreversible harmful unthinkable effects beyond the conception of their engineers. Consider the nuclear bomb, population control . . . economic policies . . . eugenics . . .

This was really fundamental to the concept of allocating limited resources to overwhelming demand in economics. The question was "Will there ever be equilibrium where supply meets demand?" It was more than economics at play; politics was into the fray of which I was glad we did not have to consider.

David Ricardo, another economist argued that there was mutual benefit from trade or barter even if one party that was resource-rich with highly skilled labour was more productive in every possible area than its trading counterpart who was resource-poor with unskilled labour, insofar as each concentrated on the activities where it had a *relative* productivity advantage. This translated to the theory of comparative advantage, a fundamental argument in favour of free trade among nations and of *specialisation* among individuals. In later years in the real world of business, I saw this at work for benefit and for disadvantage. Power often was in the hands of the few—large and/ or rich.

We had to present group projects before the class on particular topics that were relevant. My group's subject was a rather extensive one: "Will monetary union in the EEC (European Economic Community) lead to political union?" This topic required a review of the background in the formation of the European common market, and the economic policies centred in a common agricultural policy (CAP) among member countries that had evolved over time and arguing that monetary union would lead to political union. We essentially set the long paper out in several coherent parts with each team member taking a part and specialising in its delivery. From it I learnt a great deal about the interrelationships and interdependencies among history, geography, government, politics, and economics.

Macroeconomics analyses the entire economy and the factors affecting it such as inflation, unemployment, economic growth, fiscal (budgets pertaining to income and expenditure) and monetary policies (including money supply, interest rates and so on). Macroeconomics appeared as more relevant in the context of economic issues then:

economic union to monetary union in the then European Economic Community, the international currency crisis creating havoc for the U. S. dollar and the many economies pegged to it, the ensuing international debt, monetary reserves, monetary and fiscal policies, and trade flows. We each bought a little booklet by a local professor from our own Singapore University entitled "The International Economic Crisis" that explained what precipitated the then crisis all over the world.

Biology as a general subject embraced various specific branches of study: zoology, botany, and ecology. Biology was endearing as it shed light on all the life that encircled us from the bacteria, protozoa, amoeba, and the like that we could not see with the naked eye, to those large enough for us to see and observe. *Zoology* dealt with the animal kingdom including structure (embryology, classification, habits, growth, and development) and distribution. Ants, beetles, bees, moths, butterflies, birds, the earthworm, centipede, lizards, frogs, fishes, guinea pigs, cats, dogs, and the like that we have seen and touched, yet had no understanding of their behaviours, life cycles, habitats, and classifications, brought a whole new view of the massive system of the animal kingdom to the fore. *Botany* explained the primary and secondary forests, why certain plants exist in each, affected by their nature of growth, their need for nutrients and sunlight, and so on. Structures of plants and flowers, their purposes, their species were all very exciting. It was new knowledge classified and systematised. All helped in getting a view of plants and their place in nature. *Ecology* was a study of interactions of organisms with their natural environment, with each other, and with their a-biotic environments. Walking through the Clementi/Kent Ridge areas where the National University of Singapore now stood, on the natural terrain and eco system, we caught a view of ferns, the kinds of undergrowth, the Venus flytrap, and so on. It was not about plants alone, it was about life of the fauna and flora, of insects, creepy crawlies, birds, where interaction and interdependence existed among them in a sustainable environment. Shifts in elements of the eco system affected the composition of the population of animals, insects, birds, crawlies, etc within the system. *The eco system offered a microcosm of a self-managed system at work.* At Labrador, the thick carpet of dried leaves and falling twigs/branches hid a whole range of insects and worms of sorts that wriggled and scampered with a handful scoop of the top layer. They were quietly and busily at work out of human view. Those eco trips were quite exhilarating for the learning and appreciation of animals and plants in the natural. It was not an apparently dead system but one that was teeming with life unknown to the untaught and the unobservant. There was enough wonderment that made learning meaningful. Secrets in nature certainly never failed to excite the imagination.

The area of molecular biology was skimmed and a look at the DNA, their structures and functioning, made for very enlightening appreciation of the many layers of organisation within something as small as a cell. The mechanisms by which cells harness energy from their micro environment via chemical reactions are metabolism within the system and with other related systems. In the next section on chemistry, we can see the very close link between chemistry and biology. The self-organising capabilities of nature are simply glorious, from the simple as in a cell to a whole complex human system that requires perfectly coordinated sub systems within it that 'talks' not only to its members but also to those of related systems. It was all mind boggling, so highly intelligent, and certainly aeons beyond man's possible creations.

A most memorable part of biology was the human body. One way to understand the circulatory system (arteries, veins, and capillaries, and their flows), the digestive system (food tract, digestive tract, gastro-intestinal system, and excretion), the muscular, skeletal, and nervous systems, was to see the real thing. We obviously could not use a live human to work on and so there were the guinea pigs all soaked in formalin in large glass jars. They brought out an air of biting pungency that was eye-tearing whenever we worked on them. Dissecting them was not much different from that of the large frogs more regularly used. We shall shortly see.

There were times we used large frogs and these were live ones from Smith Street in Chinatown. Live ones were required so that we could better understand what went on by actually seeing the process of breathing or the blood circulation and so on. Frogs were easier to manage than guinea pigs in the context of immobilisation and holding down. One of our classmates who lived in the adjacent Temple Street area bought the frogs on behalf of all. They were jumping in plastic bags; we simply held a frog faced down in the palm of the hand with the index finger pressing down the head, the thumb on its back, the other fingers holding taut the kicking fore legs, with its underbelly resting on the palm. A large pin pushed into the pith of its central nerve just behind the head much like the spinal cord, easily paralysed it. Once paralysed, the large frog was very manageable. We laid it on a wax tray, stuck smaller pins into four legs all spread out. The frog was still alive, just simply paralysed. One could see the heart beating and pushing against the thin skin on the underbelly as they moved in tandem. Dissecting was quite straightforward as long as we had the dissecting kit ready on hand; the kit comprised the scalpel, tweezers, surgical scissors, probes (bent at thirty degrees at the end with rounded tips so as not to puncture the blood vessels etc.). Using the tweezers, the underbelly skin—usually white and a little rough—was 'pinched' and the scissors went in to incise the skin from the bottom all the way to near the neckline exposing a good view of the intestines, stomach, liver, kidney, lungs, and heart. Accidents could happen when shaking hands cut a vessel causing the specimen to appear bloodied. After a few sessions, accidents altogether ceased when steadier hands that were more experienced worked on them. The scissors made further incisions laterally at the top and bottom completely exposing the whole 'insides' of the animal. With the underbelly skin pinned to the wax tray, there was a clear view to work on the insides. We had to draw what we saw for submission as lab work. One day it was the blood circulatory system, another day was the digestive system, or the muscular-skeletal system, and so on. Biology was always interesting, lots of facts joining all the dots, and offering insight about life in nature. Mostly declarative, few considerations required, biology was much about systems in nature, and their dynamic inter-relatedness and inter-dependence in the bigger scheme of things. The cell to the organ to the system to the body of systems in the creature, to the eco-system, and to the environment at large—that was systems at work. As a declarative subject, we had no questions to ask, so when the text stated that in the course of evolution, the outcome was such and such, we took them as fact. It was as though research scientifically inquired and performed on the subject, had received agreement and approval from all the luminaries/authorities of the scientific community, and this was now fact. Here's an example of the 'hidden persuaders' at work. Perhaps advancement in science and also discoveries in time left evolution on the theory self. Early adherents of evolution in the face of new and opposing scientific evidence have become hard put to hold on to questionable hypotheses. However, the almost ubiquitous application of evolution had etched itself into the human mind through common use, acceptance, and the education process. Today in the great universities of the world, evolution hold little justifiable truth but is still valued for its original thought that shook world thinking when it was first propagated. It is a case of the old dinosaur trying to weave its way out of error not by the thinker of the hypothesis but by equally erroneous bearers of it. Perhaps time will remove it from the memories of human kind.

Chemistry is a branch of physical science that studies the composition, properties, and behaviour of matter. As it is a fundamental component of matter, the atom is the basic unit of chemistry. Chemistry is concerned with atoms and their interactions with other atoms, with particular focus on the properties of the chemical bonds formed between species. Chemistry is also concerned with the interactions between atoms or molecules and various forms of energy (e.g. photochemical reactions, oxidation-reduction reactions, changes in phases of matter, separation of mixtures, properties of polymers, etc.). Chemistry, the central science, bridges other natural sciences like physics, geology, and biology with each other. Chemistry is a branch of physical science but distinct from physics. Chemical formulae were always fun for me, they were as modelling in that they were not a straight A + B = C. One had to understand the properties, interactions, as they were all governed by 'rules' (such as acid-alkali, valences, metal or non-metal, and so on) by which reactions worked to realise the resulting product.

The course introduced us to biochemistry, inorganic, and organic chemistry. Biochemistry dealt with structures, functions, and interactions of biological macromolecules such as proteins, nucleic acids (the NA in DNA), carbohydrates, and lipids. These macromolecules are important as they provide the structure of cells and perform many functions associated with life. The chemistry of the cells depends on reactions of smaller molecules and ions. They are inorganic for example in water and metal ions, or are organic as in the amino acids used to synthesise proteins. Amino acids were the building blocks of proteins.

Physics as 'knowledge, science of nature', or 'nature' is a part of natural philosophy and a natural science that involves the study of matter and its motion through space and time, along with related concepts such as energy and force. More broadly, it is the general analysis of nature, conducted in order to understand how the universe behaves. We have heard of the famous laws that Newton discovered, others such as the Laws of Thermodynamics, and so on.

Physics is one of the oldest academic disciplines, perhaps the oldest through its inclusion of astronomy. Natural sciences emerged as unique research programs in their own right. Physics intersects with many interdisciplinary areas of research, such as biophysics and quantum chemistry, with the boundaries of physics less rigidly defined. New ideas in physics often explain the fundamental mechanisms of other sciences, while opening new avenues of research in areas such as mathematics and philosophy. We came to learn of Descartes, Copernicus, Newton, Edison, Rutherford and other illustrious thinkers who played significant contribution in developing physics.

Physics also makes significant contributions through advances in new technologies that arise from theoretical breakthroughs. For example, advances in the understanding of electromagnetism or nuclear physics led directly to the development of new products that have dramatically transformed modern day society, such as television, computers, domestic appliances, and nuclear weapons; advances in thermodynamics led to the development of industrialization; and advances in mechanics inspired the development of calculus.

Three science subjects were quite a load to carry in learning, for each subject had its own branches of study. We simply had piles of books to burrow through. I have much enjoyed the study of these subjects particularly biology. As I delved into a topic, there was this sense of excitement about wanting to look deeper, to explore more, and discover all the links and relationships. It was as a subject for understanding and enjoyment, one closely related to our own kind.

3.6 Hidden Persuaders: Populism, Political Thought

I stumbled on *The Hidden Persuaders* in the school library, and out of curiosity browsed it and found it rather interesting. I borrowed it to further review, and from this book became interested about propaganda. One thing led to another and soon I was reading about communism, political thought, and populism. First published in 1957, the author Vince Packard explored the use of consumer motivational research and other *psychological* techniques, including subliminal messages and tactics, by advertisers to manipulate expectations and induce desire for products, particularly in the American post-war era. He identified 'compelling needs' that advertisers promised products will fulfil. According to Packard, these needs were so strong that people were compelled to buy products to satisfy them. The book also explored the *manipulative* techniques of promoting politicians to the electorate. The book questioned the morality of using these techniques. The book made aware that there were so many 'silent' and 'hidden' messages that exist in the media such as the television and magazines, even the newspapers. Looking back, I realized why I had avoided certain messages such as bible prophecy and bible verses in the Plain Truth magazine for they came across clearly, as the magazine's positioning. I was not a Christian then and simply abhorred such messages. My abhorrence of Biblical quotations was really a two-edged sword: it kept me away from the light of God's word and drew me into the darkness of the world's thinking. It was unfortunate to The Plain Truth that I the unbeliever could choose to ignore the message they were propagating. Yet there were so many other messages that did not hit one hard enough to consider as a position, they ultimately had infiltrated the reader's mind, subtly subverting it in degrees, till it became acceptable just as Packard had described them as 'subliminal'. This was frightening, the very thought of it was initially a shock that these methods can be real when left in the hands of a Hitler, or Stalin or Mao where in those

times, their megalomania and/or fanaticism would stop at nothing to
control the minds of the young and old alike. My shock was that man
actually manipulated man for selfish motives through subversion of
weak minds, as I explored the process involved. Can we allow this
subversion to happen? Can we put responsible people to manage the
use of these hidden persuaders? The ultimate question turned to the
reality around us. Was the world real before the subverting messages
twisted it to the present state? Were we really free in a world that
'communicated' or persuaded to draw us to its way of thinking, to its
ideology?

Populism has been viewed as a political ideology, political philosophy,
or as a type of discourse. Generally, populists tend to claim that they
side with 'the people' against 'the elites'. I thought of it as propaganda.
While at the school library, I came across a red hard cover book with
big words in white on the front cover that read 'Populism'. Visually
attractive, the word populism was new to me, and I had been clueless
about the subject. I picked it up, browsed the contents page and the
pages that followed. It looked interesting and I borrowed it to explore
further. Populism dealt with that which appeals to the people, a
demagogy, a 'catch all' for all that was popular to the masses, to the
audience, the population at large. Was there such a thing as the will of
the people? Was democracy real? Can universal suffrage do its work
or has its work carved out by the employment of populism? Was there
really such a thing as political ideology or just politicians twisting
ideology to suit a popular position supported by the uninformed
masses?

Communism was a revolutionary socialist movement to create
a classless, moneyless, and stateless social order structured upon
common ownership of the means of production, as well as a social,
political, and economic ideology that aimed at the establishment of this
social order. This movement, in its Marxist-Leninist interpretations,

significantly influenced the history of the 20th century, which saw intense rivalry between the 'socialist world' (socialist states ruled by communist parties) and the 'western world' (countries with capitalist economies). It was a rather divisive subject that even at home, in my family and the state, often evoked riotous commotion in discussion or discourses that drew sharp distinctions with the common man coffee shop armchair 'political ideologues'. Marxist theory held that *pure communism* inevitably emerged from the development of the productive forces that led to a superabundance of material wealth, allowing therefore, for distribution based on need and social relations based on freely associated individuals. We often think of communism interchangeably as socialism; however, Marxism contended that socialism was a transition on the road to communism. Leninism added a variation to Marxism in the notion of a vanguard party to lead the proletarian revolution and to secure all political power after the revolution, for the working class, in order to develop a universal class consciousness and worker participation, in a transitional stage between capitalism and communism. Perhaps, we can think of Che Guevara as Marxist-Leninist while Castro was political communist. Realism moderated idealism; idealism adjusted by politics. Can there ever be real communism?

'Hidden Persuaders', populism, communism and political thoughts were coincidental in my time and age. They simply converge as a piece of history for that epoch. It was the era of the Cuban missile crisis—Kennedy-Khrushchev, the Vietnam War—Kennedy-Johnson-Nixon, and everything else was about a bi-polar USA and the USSR, the Cold War, of tensions and détente. It was a time of extremities. It precipitated a social malaise, disillusionment in that *present* time and yet an unsettling lack of assurance, a languid restlessness when looking into the *future* of its time.

Added to this might be George Orwell, known for his book *Animal Farm* among others that I had studied at the age of sixteen as part of my English Literature course. He was also a novelist and journalist, and wrote literary criticism, fiction, and poetry. His works clearly spoke of an awareness of social injustice, an opposition to totalitarianism, and a commitment to democratic socialism. 'Orwellian' with a reference to him had come to connote an attitude and a policy of control, propaganda, of denial of the past, misinformation, surveillance, changing history of the past by expunging them from public records, and so on. Orwell believed there was a close association between bad prose and ideology: "In our time, political speech and writing are largely the defence of the indefensible. Things like the continuance of British rule in India, the Russian purges and deportations, the dropping of the atom bombs on Japan, can indeed be defended, but only by arguments which are too brutal for most people to face, and which do not square with the professed aims of political parties. Thus, political language has to consist largely of euphemism, question-begging and sheer cloudy vagueness. Defenceless villages are bombarded from the air, the inhabitants driven out into the countryside, the cattle machine-gunned, the huts set on fire with incendiary bullets: this is called pacification. Millions of peasants are robbed of their farms, and sent trudging along the roads with no more than they can carry: this is called transfer of population or rectification of frontiers. People are imprisoned for years without trial, or shot in the back of the neck or sent to die of scurvy in Arctic lumber camps: this is called elimination of unreliable elements. Such phraseology is needed if one wants to name things without calling up mental pictures of them."

3.7 School Band

The band had always had a huge space in my school life and continued to be so in the two years in pre-university. It was an enjoyable period when one had learned the technical aspects of the instrument and music well enough to not labour at them. Proficiency created more room for enjoyment of the music as handling technicalities became second nature. I left the St. John Ambulance Band as time became scarce and the need for alternative music learning was less needful; making music in an alternative environment was nevertheless a sure pleasure due to the different focus and theme.

I became the band quarter master, one who took care of the logistics such as issue of uniform and the accessories as lanyards, epaulettes, metal buttons, waste bands, caps, and badges—surely elements reminiscent of the traditional ceremonial garb of an era past. The care and maintenance of musical instruments was generally important as we expected instrumentalists to care for their personal instrument in protecting its serviceability, cleaning them after practices, and informing us of any damage or a need for repair. I would arrange with a regular vendor to evaluate the degree of servicing or change of parts, request a quotation for submission to the teacher-in-charge before proceeding with the recommended actions. Things did not move as quickly as in today's environment, the turnaround from time of order to final delivery could take weeks.

3.8 A Slice of Life

People and things make life very liveable; they teach us a great deal about nature, particularly human nature; about relationships, the way people think, and behave and what drives them. Truly, they are all very much a reflection of us in varying shades and degrees.

Probably my last photo at the old RI with Capitol Theatre on the right
in the background and behind me was the Stamford Canal with St.
Andrew's Cathedral after Stamford Road. I believe we were having
some marching practice with our musical instruments and a friend
took a posed shot. It was wonderful to play in the large open space
and to hear the trumpet blare float about the air, far and high.

They are slices of our lives. We can all be diversely *different* and yet at the same time very closely *similar*. The author has no intention in offering critiques on people or particular persons; their names mentioned are fictitious but their characters are real. There are passing comments made with no malice or a sense of it, merely just to offer the reader a sense of all those about him, and the flavours with which they laced him.

HBL liked to crack crude jokes, sometimes rather gross. He wrote and drew in bold short straight lines much like an architect. A look at his signature and you immediately knew that was HBL. He loved photography and has a plethora of personal equipment. Naturally, he shot for the Rafflesian Times, the school's newsletter. You might think of him as a creative sort not quite a liberal fine artist but someone who had a structured creativity if there was such a word for it. His less than flowing oral stuttering and staccato articulations were like his structured creativity. Clearly, HBL kept within a narrow band of thinking, his interests capped within that band and structure: predictable as his lines were.

EL was from a convent school, the tallest girl in class, wore an almost perpetual natural smile that pushed up and accentuated her cheeks, bespectacled, straight haired tied into two pony tails at the back of her head. On all accounts, EL was generally girlish and wore a typically pretty Teochew disposition, her two front mildly bunny teeth were definitive but did not overshadow or impose on her pleasant facial appearance. Endowed with a rather intelligent straight forward nature with little interest or stamina for long and deep intellectual arguments, easy and happy sort: academically, an achiever. Eventually she went to university to become a doctor.

SL spoke with a foreign accent as though she was from Australia. Her family lived in a private landed property, rather casual in relationships, socially and politically correct with all in the correct circles, quite unknowable, loved the limelight, and stood out easily from her size and obvious demand for social space. SL went on to Australia on a scholarship and became a surgeon.

SK was always careful without appearing so. Ever extroverted and chatty, there was little that anyone could fathom about him. We first met when we were in secondary three and became buddies. Apart from some naughty secrets of his, there was not a thing that would tell me of his true person even though we were friendly and respectful of each other. we corresponded for a time when he went to Australia on a scholarship to study medicine.

YG had always an emotional baggage—not his own but probably inherited from his taxi driver father—that apparently hung on him in all his dealings. It had never departed from him even after nearly forty years, that is, up until today; I never could understand how he failed to see the baggage. Not a brilliant person, YG seemed to know how to make the grade. He was one who would not leave the scene of a political fray; he was instinctively as one who wanted in on the action just for the action. His ideology was not convincing, not original. That historical emotional baggage seemed to hold him down refusing him to seize the opportunities and rise above himself.

Truly, I was without wise counsel when the will was weak and dragged about to succumb to passions of the heart, and in adolescence necessarily precipitated restlessness. Tossing about in the raging currents of growing up confuses the spirit's sensibility to reality.

4.

At Eighteen—Frustration

Without counsel purposes are disappointed:
but in the multitude of counsellors they are established.
—Proverbs 15:22

Two years might seem like too short a time for adjustments and was a bit like 'do or do not'. Some amount of frustration came in the way of the private focus on accountancy studies that were quite diverse from the pre-medicine studies in school. A new love for writing poetry derailed my priorities; continued indulgence in trumpet music, and the hunger to read every interesting and thought provoking literature took out the wind from studies proper. In the tug-of-war, I failed to balance my priorities between the high volume of relevant work that mattered to complete and the pleasure of delving into things that did not matter. Such folly exacerbated restlessness. Truly, I was without wise counsel when the will was weak and dragged about to succumb to passions of the heart, and in adolescence necessarily precipitated restlessness. Tossing about in the raging currents of growing up confuses the spirit's sensibility to reality.

4.1 Presentation on Buddhism Presented Problems

The General Paper teacher requested me to present a paper on Buddhism to the class in one of her sessions, as I was a Buddhist. The teacher was wife to a Methodist priest. There was sufficient time to prepare for the presentation and the subject was one I have studied since childhood, professed to believe in, practiced, and shared with others. The subject was supposedly familiar, the preparation naturally easy. I would talk about the history from the Prince Siddharta Gautama to his encounters with the state of humans he saw during his ride through the streets of Nepal: a birth, a beggar, an ascetic, the sick, the ailing and ageing, and the dead as expressed in the dirge of mourning. This moved him to think that man must traverse these conditions of human sufferings and of separation from society. He discovered and taught how man could wind out of these vicious cycles: through meditation on 'nothingness' to attain perfect bliss (nirvana) that would free one from these earthly woes.

Someone raised a very literal question of how one could attain nirvana. That set me in a bit of a fix. Nirvana had always been a difficult subject; there simply was never a definition of it. It was supposedly a state or condition where enlightened, one experienced no sense of anxiety as though free from the fetters of earthly and reincarnated life. I managed to explain through a corollary that served to clear the doubt in the question. My answer was superficial in treating the question. However, it truly caused a revival in my dissatisfaction with the whole concept of nirvana. It fundamentally had to do with putting a beginning to life and having an answer as to its end, to which nirvana offered nothing definitive. The disillusionment never went away and bugged me through to my National Service years until I met Jesus Christ. Knowledge of the world, in the wisdom of man kills the truth; the way of God lifts the spirit. *For I determined not to know any thing among you, save Jesus Christ, and him crucified. And I was with you in weakness, and in fear, and in much trembling. And my speech and my preaching was not with enticing words of man's wisdom, but in demonstration of the Spirit and of power: That your faith should not stand in the wisdom of men, but in the power of God. Howbeit we speak wisdom among them that are perfect: yet not the wisdom of this world, nor of the princes of this world, that come to nought:*—1 Corinthians 2:6-9.

But the natural man receiveth not the things of the Spirit of God: for they are foolishness unto him: neither can he know them, because they are spiritually discerned.—1 Corinthians 2:14.

4.2 Alternative Music—Jazz

Dixieland music was a style of jazz music developed in New Orleans and is one of the earliest styles of jazz. Dixie referred to the Civil War southern states, at that time known as 'The Old South'. The definitive sound of Dixieland jazz was the trumpet, which played the tune or melody, or paraphrase with the other 'front line' instruments such as the trombone and clarinet improvising around that melody. This 'overlaying' effect produced beautiful polyphonic sounds that sort of filled up the space each front line instrument created in the paraphrasing. The support section usually includes the double bass, piano, and drums. Louis Armstrong's band was most popular for Dixieland jazz; his influence, however, cuts through all of jazz. My one and only exposure to Dixieland jazz was from a book entitled Dixieland Blues that had some twenty five scores of such music. Playing was very fun and lively and it was sometime later that I actually went on to listen to something close to the real thing at a music records store. That alone helped improve my appreciation when the 'front line' instruments and support section brought the music to life. Much of my learning came from reading and playing scores and listening to recorded material.

It was some years later that I had an opportunity to watch Acker Bilk live at the DBS Auditorium. He was a jazz clarinettist and noted for his rendition of Moon River and Autumn Leaves. The jazz that Bilk played was decades after the traditional jazz era. Of course, with an accompanying band, they took on jazz that had transitioned out of the traditional hot jazz popularised by Armstrong. Listening to a real band had to be multiple times better than just trying to interpret scores or listen to recorded versions. *Take this lesson on listening into our lives, is it not so that in listening with knowledge we learn? Those most akin to tinkle as cymbals to interpret than to first learn and listen, often miss the opportunity to learn. Listen with a heart, I urge you my readers.* When I worked as a senior executive at a U.S. multinational company some two decades later, I had an opportunity to visit a jazz bar in Union Station in downtown Tulsa, Oklahoma, to listen to regular and jam sessions over a drink. *Another lesson in listening to music that I learnt was to understand the emotions they stir up in us.* The emotions affect the way of our thinking and hence of our reasoning. This can mean clear thinking or one shrouded in shades that could then in turn affect the decisions we make. That sounds like theory until one sits in a jazz bar to realise how the music can have a powerful effect over us in those few hours or for that matter at a piano recital or listening to a symphony orchestra. According to our disposition, jazz music can variously evoke our sensibilities from the pleasurable emotions, the soothing touches, the sentimental undertones, the sensual subtlety, the libertarian overtones, the rebellious urgings, and so on. Music is a channel, a form to allow our craving to express ourselves. This craving to express emotions draw us away from reality and ensconce us in the couch of escapism that eventually directs us to idolise persona or forms of music; they entangle us to the point of worship and separate us from the truth. *Mortify therefore your members which are upon the earth; fornication, uncleanness, inordinate affection, evil concupiscence, and covetousness, which is idolatry.—* Colossians 3:5.

4.3 Cannot comprehend Comprehension

My General Paper (GP) teacher had noticed I seemed somewhat to fare poorly in comprehension but was able to be tops for composition or essay. When you put the two together: an A1 in composition, plus a near fail in comprehension I could only manage a B3. The good thing was that composition had a higher weightage than comprehension. My grading stayed that way throughout the two years in Pre-university. Tried hard as the teacher did, I never did too well at comprehension and so my grade for GP hovered in the B3 and A2 range. I could not explain or understand my problem if there was one. The score at comprehension told me there was a problem but my essay was always in reasonably perfect English. Did I have a problem comprehending English? It had always remained an enigma to me.

4.4 Prime Minister Lee Kuan Yew's Daughter

We met for the first time when I approached her for her signature in an attempt to collect as many signatures of the seniors in one of several competitions for the upcoming prom. She was a year my senior. The prom was organised for new entrants to pre-university one so everyone got to know everyone else. Of course, as we all know that was never the case with all the noise and partying, students clustering among themselves and so on. I walked into a pre-university two class where the din was deafening as the boisterous students chatted and laughed without restraint while awaiting their teacher. In the old RI buildings still, with the high ceilings and poor acoustics, the cacophony was loudly cantankerous. In the midst of all the casual activities, there was this girl with short straight hair who reminded me of my second sister, Zhu. She was at her two feet by two feet square desk, poring over a mightily thick book totally engrossed in her reading. What a scene—stillness in a storm or a marketplace—she was as though oblivious to all about her, locked into her own world. I recognised her; she was none other than Wei Ling, our then Prime Minister's daughter. I walked up to her and asked for her signature. She did not look up, took the card from me, and simply signed the Chinese character of 'Ling' for her name. She pushed the card back to me, I took it up, thanked her, and walked off. That scene will always stick in my mind. In that few short moments, I caught an enduring glimpse of discipline, of an attitude honed by years of habit and training. Much I could write about it.

In the days following, often by coincidence I watched from my top floor classroom at the end of the school day, a Mercedes pulling up to the car park. A lady came out and waited a little while and Wei Ling would pass her the files or bag, and went off for to return some while later. The lady was probably a governess or bodyguard . . . just my guess. There were other times Wei Ling would be running alone round the school's new tartan tracks. She was incidentally a strong middle distance runner for RI if my memory served me right. These were the times I had stayed back at school for band practice or logistics administration; I was the band's quarter master.

In my earlier book, I had met her older brother Hsien Loong who was drum major for the Catholic High school band. Wei Ling reminded of him: lonely, standing out of the group, not that she was aloof but she was isolated. Perhaps she, like her brother, was avoided by those around them rather than they the others. Life must have seemed unusual to segregate from others in a like setting for possible reasons of protective physical security and privacy of sort because one's father is the prime minister. Perhaps having siblings was a perfect solution, a threesome circle of children each not so far apart in age as was the case here, would have made life quite normal at home. Wei Ling had a younger brother.

4.5 Keynes: something Macro

'Stonier and Hague', these were the last names of two authors of a textbook on macroeconomics. The teacher made all references to it by 'Stonier and Hague' to the point I cannot recall now the actual title of the book. Perhaps it was 'A Textbook in Economics'. Pretty unfriendly looking book, with the ELBS (English Low-priced Book Series for the benefit of British Commonwealth countries) soft covers, one-toned dirty green, with cheap thick but light buff newsprint in between. There were no photos or colours inside just black printing ink. Mathematical formulae were in many places when one flipped through the pages. Call it a 'dry' book in appearance until one went through its pages with studied intent, and some things started to come alive. This book that I was so afraid to open in the first instance because it was rather thick, its appearance Spartan, and uninviting became one of my favourite economics text books. There was a distinctive clear straightforward approach and style of writing that endeared me to it.

4.6 Philosophy: Reasoning in Argument

As part of the General Paper subject the teacher cursorily exposed us to certain concepts such as logic, deductive/ inductive thinking, syllogism, reasoning, arguments, premise and so on. It was like an introduction to philosophy, the study of general and fundamental problems, such as those connected with reality, existence, knowledge, values, reason, mind, and language; distinguished from other ways of addressing such problems by its critical, generally systematic approach and its reliance on rational argument. The affectation of reasoning smothers the conscience. To address intangible problems and concepts in limited words that express the sense of, the feeling of, a solution to, is at best theory and hypothesis. I remembered having to write an essay on Descartes' famous *Cogito ergo sum* 'I think, therefore I am'.

I did it with little passion for the argument, and treated it more as an exercise in application of the context of the lesson taught. Trying to put an understanding to 'think' was in itself a massive problem; to argue it meant acceptance of a regular understanding of thinking in the context of it as a function of the brain that required the coming together of multiple factors or elements. The argument can take different possible shapes depending on one's starting point and definitions of the points of the argument. As you are reading this, you could possibly be thinking that I am writing some mumbo jumbo, and you are *probably* right till I challenge you. Let us leave it at that . . . it is a trivial exercise of our faculties, absolutely no realisable truth from the process. *Should a wise man utter vain knowledge, and fill his belly with the east wind? Should he reason with unprofitable talk? Or with speeches wherewith he can do no good?*—Job 15:2-3.

4.7 End of Pre-University

Having been through two years of Pre-University, I concluded that they were useful to the development of my mind and person. It was not simply about the preparation for a set career in some professional field. It was still in a sense a general education that exposed one to an approach to learning, to problem solving of a different kind, to thinking about the issues around us that were real, that whipped up our passions or smothered our disinterest. I believe that the Pre-University years challenged my agitated mind, raised my level of awareness of the issues of the society we lived in, and heightened my response to them. Just thinking and feeling about them engaged me in spirit to the point of penning them in my essays both private and public. I was never vocal about them, I was still turning them about in my mind, they have not yet taken on a clear form and thoroughly conceptualised. With the seeds of questioning sown, it would take time to sink the roots.

. . . Pre-University days (time) were an important piece in my personal growth and development, and had provided a rich ground (space) for seeds of discovery to take root and flourish; for the seeds of restlessness to fester and search the way forward. A mere two years supported by all the years before to take one into a real adult world where execution would dominate in translating thoughts and affections to visible outcomes.

My conclusion has been that the Pre-University days (time) were an important segment in my personal growth and development, and had provided a rich ground (space) for seeds of *discovery* to take root and flourish; of *restlessness* to fester and search for the way forward. A mere two years supported by all the years before to take one into a real adult world where execution would dominate in translating thoughts and affections to visible outcomes. Learning by letters was certainly a powerful way by which we accumulate knowledge for to do so by experience in a short life of four score years would undoubtedly be impossible. Letters with every available opportunity for experience would speed up appreciation and understanding of the complexities circling our lives. Knowledge itself is quite worthless, man's knowledge is less than perfect, relative, gradually acquired and accumulated, is largely fraught with opinion, preference, and error; appropriately and usefully applied we bring knowledge to bear, in its application and in its insight. Still, it is limited. Intellectual knowledge is really condemned when it cannot provide a premise for its purports, truly deplorable. On the other hand, God's knowledge is perfect, is absolute, inerrant, embracing all past, present, and the future, it is intuitive, and searches the innermost heart and thought of man. *The fear of the LORD is the beginning of wisdom: a good understanding have all they that do his commandments: his praise endureth for ever.*—Psalm 111:10. *The fear of the LORD is the beginning of wisdom: and the knowledge of the holy is understanding.*—Proverbs 9:10.

I have never seriously considered the 'protection' of Singapore as fundamental to National Service. We were to be a deterrent force for an 'upstart' nation. If we were unable to inflict a fighting bite let's despatch our offender a warning scratch.

5.

Time for National Service

*I beseech you therefore, brethren, by the mercies of God, that ye present your bodies
a living sacrifice, holy, acceptable unto God, which is your reasonable service.*
—Romans 12:1

S ervice may often be thought as a giving to another; National
Service as a giving of a brief two years or two and a half years
to the nation, a time mapped out from one's life of four score
years, and one might venture to think it was but a teeny tiny sacrifice.
It did not remove; it simply separated and marked out distinctly on
the canvas of our lives. Yes, service is truly a sacrifice; not as a *handing
out*. It is a *giving up* of oneself to a cause, albeit mandatory, to serve
in obedience to a national will. It was this service, this sacrifice that
took us from the receiving end of our youthful lives to that of the
service to another, our nation, and all that it embraces. It is truly
rather remarkable to think of service as sacrifice for each connotes
and therefore draws from us different emotions and responses to
dealing with National Service. The motive all at once becomes clear
that the sacrifice is a consecration to the higher and nobler national

purpose, akin to what the Chinese refer to the Big 'I' (other-centred) and not the small 'I' (self-centred). It is in the service of sacrifice, we move from boys to men; and in the giving, we gain.

I was all excited about entering the armed forces not so much about the National Service idea. National Service was a mandatory government service in the Armed Forces (air, land, and sea) that took young men soon after their formal education, typically at eighteen years of age. They then served two years or two and half years to prepare them to become operationally ready to undertake war in the event of an attack on our nation. We never quite understood its purpose other than those parroted by government propaganda, which if I were to believe, National Service must prove to be excellent in its execution to achieve that high sounding purpose. I looked forward to it, rather excited to become a soldier, an officer, a man who would be adequately prepared to raise an offensive in defence of our families and country in the event of an external encroachment of our peace. I have never seriously considered the 'protection' of Singapore as fundamental to National Service. We were to be a deterrent force for an 'upstart' nation. If we were unable to inflict a fighting bite let's send our offender a warning scratch. Singapore had a very small regular army that would not be able to adequately resist enemy attacks, hence enlistment of an army of young men served to supplement the regular army. The two years or two and a half years for some, were to prepare young men to be operationally ready to enter into combat when the need arose. The Americans called it the draft and the British, conscription. For our purpose, I shall call it NS enlistment. In its early years of establishment, Singapore relied on Israeli expertise and experience to guide the workings of the national service scheme. I supposed there were parallels drawn between Singapore and Israel. In geography, Israel was land locked and Singapore was an island surrounded by immediate neighbouring nations of Malaysia and Indonesia. Politically and historically, Israel had Islamic nations for its neighbours; Singapore similarly endowed with Islamic nations for its immediate neighbours.

5.1 Preparations for NS enlistment

When it was near the end of the two-year pre-university programme, I physically prepared for National Service with a two-week stint as a sanitary/plumbing apprentice at a construction work site where work generally required much strength and endurance. Two weeks were never enough. However, I had a young lifetime of much physical activities that kept me fit except for a smaller frame that offered less muscle mass for great and enduring strength. In short, I could harness strength for short bursts of time but was unable to keep it up for longer. It was more of grit and determination than of natural physical strength. Waking up early in the morning, getting to the work site, carrying heavy tool pails up the sloping grounds where the constructed buildings were, mixing sand and cement with the manual spade, and suffering from the cement bite on the hands, while lifting large manufactured steel plates for the roof water tanks was demanding. These morning routines were quite some work for my small and skinny frame. Still, pulling in to the roof landing steel plates lifted by a crane on the ground was dangerous work. There was no safety belt to attach to an anchor or holding structure on the roof, nor had we safety helmets or boots; we depended on ingenuity and common sense. In those days, work safety standards were the bare minimum, very deplorable.

Digging the grounds—with mid-sized tools as changkuls or mattocks—to create a channel to lay clay sewage pipes for temporary toilets—chipping bricks to serve as supports for the pipes, laying the hemp round the clay pipe joints to serve as gaskets of sort—was as the manual work of a foreign construction worker today. The round clay pipes were four inches in inner diameter, about a foot and a half long with a slight taper at one end. At the wider end, a much wider cup or bowl of two and a half inches deep shaped to hold the tapered end of another similar pipe to simulate a gasket jointing packed with hemp and cement in the cup to secure the jointing. These clay pipes, glazed on the outside surface appeared as brittle yet by its design and construction were fit for use as sewer pipes for temporary toilets. Buried in shallow earth away from heavy human and work traffic, for short-term use to be removed and discarded when the construction work on the main property was completed, these pipes served their purpose. As the finger lifting that which it can, the palm even more than what the finger can, and the hand according to its stronger ability, there is proportionate application. We each have our portion according to what life metes out to us.

At the end of each work day, I would be so exhausted and fell asleep at the dinner table at home. Such was the case where the physical exertions exceeded the load that a physical frame would structurally permit. The physical strains and fatigue shut out all else in the mind, something of a big lesson that was soon to help me in my National Service stint. What I also learned was that the earnings were meagre as an apprentice at five dollars a day. The breakfast, tea and coffee breaks at mid morning and afternoon, and the lunch hour sucked all the earnings and more. My mother had to supplement my takings in advance, as I did not receive payment until two weeks into the work. It was as though a young man sold his life for five dollars a day. His life was as nothing . . . waking early, jostling with others, and travelling to work in a rumbling pick-up truck still tired from the day before, hefting the heavy tools up the hillock, digging or ditching the earth, working in constrained spaces, knocking, chipping, mixing sand and cement, threading metal pipes. At the end of the day, too tired to even keep his eyes open at dinner, it was to the bed till dawn. In common jargon, he saw not the sunrise or the sunset. Worse still, he could not make out day and night, simply going through a cycle of waking and sleeping, and waking and sleeping. More importantly his mind was 'drugged and sewn up' by the physical strains such that no space was available for the mind to add substance and meaning to every single day. Perhaps in time past dictators have harnessed the strength of man to work him as they did the beasts, of ox and ass; that left out any room for any ingenious designs that could free man. Man became a captive of his own strength. As prisoners that worked the oars in a ship's galley, man caught up in the grind can often be prisoners to others and to the world. The deplorable workhouses of old days and the inhumanity of prisons were no less similar in concept. This was not the kind of work that he would look forward to do when weighing the effort and the compensation. At the same time, compensation was apparently time-based regardless of the effort and/or ingenuity employed in its performance or the quality of its output. The measure or yardstick of work in those sense mentioned, was inequitable. He cared for having a sound and fair value measure of his employable skills and knowledge, and the applicable amount of work for the task performed.

The demands of society for growth and success likewise draw man to its grind. Man loses his contentment in the simple and humble for the glamorous and flashy allures of the world, whether by force or in coveting them. The short stint in construction offered the author an understanding of one extreme where the body loses total control, putting to sleep both mind and body. Man can become a zombie, the worst kind of zombie, an unthinking one, and eventually losing the ability to think. It is as a walking dead, manipulated and exploited for the most nightmarish of evil possibilities. Translated to a different level of matter over the mind, where we usually talk only about 'mind over matter', we can similarly draw parallels between the temporal and eternity, the transient and permanent, the dot and the circle, the earthly and the heavenly, and so on. There is a grave warning sense for vigilance over the mind, over our thoughts, our affections, and our walk or conduct of life; and also of the violation of the body for work or for corruption.

Mental preparedness for the worst and for the exciting challenge of discipline in the Armed Forces, the physical preparation as apprentice at building construction, as well as his ability in running, made for a comfortable cruise in the first three months of basic military (BMT). His expectation of heavy military drill and discipline was present but in his view was without the due and proper manner of execution. There was certain lack of fairness, a sort of abuse, and a sad humiliation pervaded within the military environment that was unnecessary and yet allowed to exist. The language differential between English and Chinese had exacerbated some of these happenings and he felt quite helpless for several of his colleagues. He felt a deep sense of anger that ate into his original high-minded view of the Armed Forces. His dream was shattered somewhat, disappointment brewed and gnawed away at his military aspirations. At some point in the three months of BMT, he received an order to attend an officer cadet training (OCT) interview at the Ministry of Defence (Mindef). He openly rejected the idea of becoming an officer and made no effort to hide his disappointments in front of the high ranking panel of military interviewers. That position remained unchanged throughout National Service. Although he had a few similar requests to attend OCT interviews, he chose to skip them all.

5.2 At CMPB and Off to 5SIR

It was all of a lonely send off. He had requested it to be so; he was glad for it to be that way. He did not know what to expect but was all prepared for the worst, for the unknown. He was the oldest boy in the family and there was no forerunner before him, no comfort of knowing ahead of the real thing. He needed to find out for himself. He had prepared in the physical in terms of strength (as apprentice in the construction work site in Mandai), and in stamina (the long evening runs in the neighbourhood of Bishopsgate/Jervois area) to brace for the mental (this was the unknown). The preconception was that if one could make it through the physical, there was no mental hurdle to overcome. Had one been unable to physically overcome the demands, then one's mind had to deal with 'mind over matter' issues of failure and depression.

The 5th Singapore Infantry Regiment (5 SIR) was commonly known as Slim Barracks—after a General Slim of the British Military in India—or Portsdown Camp after the road that led to the camp. These were remnants of the old British presence from whom the Singapore Armed Forces took over, in the wake of her independence from British colonial rule and administration.

5.3 Three-month BMT

The BMT stint was mostly manageable as long as one was able to receive, give, and act accurately on instructions. However, physical fitness was the basis to make for a pleasant BMT stint. I was more than prepared and fared well.

Our **barracks** were in the block called El Alamein, a city on the northern coast of Egypt along the Mediterranean Sea. British forces were once there, as Churchill wrote after the Second World War, "Before Alamein we never had a victory. After Alamein, we never had a defeat." The grounds of the 5th Singapore Infantry Regiment reeked of the relic of the British in World War II.

Mie and family visited Portsdown camp at the end of the second week while confined to barracks. This was an ordeal in that I had to queue in the evening in a long beeline of recruits trying similarly to make a call home on a single coin-a-phone in the canteen. Mobile phones did not then exist, and for recruits to NS, to hear the voice of family on the other end of the line was a huge joy. That one call I made home gave Mie an assurance that I was well, not bruised or beaten up. It offered an opportunity to enquire after everyone's well-being at home. My sisters were possibly in the background anxious to know how I was doing. That was the great benefit of being the first in the family to enter the army. Mie passed the phone to Cai as I gave instructions on the location, visiting hours, what she can bring in, and other administrative matters. Several of my RI classmates, mostly the girls, who were young women by then, and a few of the guys who had a later enlistment, also paid a visit.

Burning shoe caps was, in my opinion, the most difficult part in the whole of my National Service although I worked on them only during that first three months of BMT. The shine never seemed adequately perfect: the near perfect roundedness without a single un-flattened pimple on the surface of a brand new pair of virgin boots in order that the reflection of my face does not contort. I had always taken great pride in this work of taking a brand new pair of boots complete with the rough pimples or if you look it on the inverse, dimples, and transforming them into completely flat shining surfaces that were simply a delight to look at and march in. That was it, that shining pair of boots or what we termed 'parade' boots were special, carried that tag, and always stood proudly in the wardrobe (we called them the more appropriate 'cabinets', rusty dark military green metal cupboards) when not in use and donned with pride for the parade square or special duties. I spent nights without sleep after the lights were put out, heating up a metal spoon over a candle, pressing it on every dimple on the boots' surface—there were thousands of them! It was worth the trouble. It was truly an art; the science came along after art had shown the way. Think of it as Michel Angelo at his sculpturing . . . Robin at his parade boots! Read Irving Stone's 1961 book on Michel Angelo's life aptly titled "The Agony and The Ecstasy" to enjoy a glimpse of the sculptor and painter's perspectives in his art. Due to the hard presses applied on the boot caps, I received many self-inflicted scalds from the hot burning spoons that skidded off them, sometimes from too much pressure, and at other times for nodding off from fatigue and sleepiness. National Service enlistees today would have missed this experience completely since the SAF discontinued the practice of shining boot caps in a long while. What on the surface might have seemed like a waste of time or of little value was truly special for those who have put in the long hours of the boot work, just putting in the hard hot presses followed by the fine and delicate touches. The joy I remembered vividly was of seeing my image in smart number three uniform with the metal insignia, cap badge, and my face reflecting from the shining boot cap as though it was a mirror on black surface. It was so smooth and well maintained that even a speck of dust would not gently light on the spotless effort.

Washing and laundry was important due to the inadequate number of sets of uniform issued. There was the brand new set for drill purposes (we called this Number 3 uniform) and therefore had to be well-starched—not too thickly yet perfectly crisp as a thin Indian cracker—and well pressed. The lower part of the long sleeves pushed inwards all the way up to the shoulder so that the long sleeve became half in length, the middle of the folded long sleeve was then crisply pressed to allow another fold up on the outside to perfectly fit just where the arm bent. This Number 3 hung on large shirt hangers and left in the cupboard, worn only for parade and drills. We also received two sets of Number 4 uniforms, one regular and the other was 'sub-standard'. I was the only one to get a slightly oversized yellowing, with 'butterfly collars, and heavy set. In one of pictures, you will think that I came out of the World War I or II. Without my spectacles and donning a fierce and tired look, I could be mistaken for a seasoned dust-beaten warrior.

Sleep was often short in the early days at Portsdown camp, curtailed to enable the shining of boot caps, washing of uniforms and ironing them. Cleaning rifles—lock stock and barrel—was also time consuming requiring much care with the shining spiralling barrel that must have no speck of dirt or dust which the instructors would call 'elephants' or 'spiders'. Such discipline in rifle cleaning stressed the importance in maintaining a highly serviceable tool that could mean life and death in combat. Food was typical with bread, a scoop of margarine or kaya, two eggs hard-boiled, and coffee or tea. They added further dullness to the already bonded life in camp, etc.

Tactical training at Clementi/Kent Ridge was suitable for particular types of tactics/movements due to the wide open land, and light secondary forest of a sort. Lots of ferns, a good uniform terrain for testing the judgement of distances, of locating positions using the clock system, served to master the basics that were applied in actual tactical manoeuvres instructing mates or men to move to, for example, a location at 10 o'clock 50 metres away. With the kind of vegetation, quite burnt and scrubby, we learned camouflage with the natural fauna, the effects of movements, facial colouring of our faces, etc. with the purpose of blending into the environment to prevent easy detection.

Live firing at the ranges occurred in progressive stages beginning with the dry shooting, that is, without live rounds, at twenty five metres. Here we used the concept of convergence of three tries being pencil marked on the target by another soldier, and allowed us to fine tune our accuracy in shooting before heading to shooting in restricted live ranges at fifty metres, then a hundred in prone, kneeling, and standing positions. These live range exercises became a regular process early on in training in order to secure an immersed understanding of shooting, the performance of man and behaviour of his machine, the rifle. For a well-trained soldier, the rifle is his wife (we took an oath on this), ever with him (except when cleaned and returned to the armoury), ever honed for battle, and performed perfectly in accordance with its purpose.

Bayonet training always began with the preliminary rifle exercises to strengthen the arms through holding the rifle round its neck and also around the barrel's end lifting the whole of the rifle's weight by the barrel's end. This was probably the most challenging as the manner offered no leverage and depended on sheer muscle strength. In one of the training, we were to hold the rifle without bayonet in firm positions and the instructors went around the platoon to test how fast the rifles held with each man. An instructor pulled at one and that rifle went with him causing the rifle sight to hit at his cheek, and blood came out shooting therefrom. He rushed to the camp medical centre for attention, returning a short while later, with a gauze patch taped over his left cheek.

Every time we had bayonet fighting sessions, we would wrap our personal issue of green army towel around the thin Bakelite hand guard of the rifle so that it does not crack from arm-to-arm parrying and butting. The Bakelite material was not a suitable one as it was too smooth and would slip from the desired parrying position. For training purposes, the towel was useful to prevent such slip although that was not the intention. Bayonet fighting had its value when in close combat; however, its importance did not lie there. Rather, it impressed in trainees a sense of survival by aggression from the shouts in charging at a target with intent to kill, the forceful parrying to kill and avoid being killed, and the ruthless thrusts into sand bags and pulling out, thrusting again, and finally inflicting the deadly thrust and turn. In the military environment of my time where automatic rifles were the norm, encounters of arm-to-arm fighting were unlikely. Even if there were such encounters, a soldier would first reach for the trigger.

with BMT section mates at a corner of the parade square at Portsdown Camp. This is where One-North is today. I was in the centre and kneeling.

5.4 Further Three-month SSL at SAFTI

My results at the 3-month BMT were commendable. As a natural progression, I went on to the School of Section Leaders at SAFTI. From there I supposed nearly all would aspire to become officers unless one is physically unfit or is likely to struggle to cope physically and hence the mental demands of the training. This was where mind over matter was severely tested. The common saying that 'the spirit is willing but the flesh is weak' has its truth in this physical sense. For a fighting fit soldier, the first basic requirement had to be the establishment of physical strength so that the retention of mental strength and acuity remain accessible to size up operational situations and to execute the appropriate moves when called upon.

The six-mile run was the equivalent of today's ten kilometre run. The running gear included a steel helmet with inner liner, a webbing with canvas pouches to contain an aluminium bottle that sat in an aluminium mess tin (for food), first aid dressing, and magazine (for bullets but no bullets for a run). There was also the bayonet in its scabbard, an AR-15 rifle hung from one shoulder or slung across the body, and heavy combat boots. That all made for a heavy run over six miles. The steel helmet was heavy relative to today's much lighter version made of synthetic Kevlar material. The aluminium filled to the brim with tap water was a real burden. Not everyone handled the run well. There was a trial run before the real one where the time clocked decided the pass/fail mark. In the trial run, he ran with a weak runner who was concerned about failing. They were section mates and he helped pace him. They ended among the last few to reach the finish line. He considered the pacing as an encouragement for his section mate, to let him set aside his lack of ability, fitness, and hence confidence to be willing to take the challenge. It was near impossible to raise fitness overnight yet encouragement can often raise a flicker of hope that may create possibilities; it was better to try than do nothing.

At the final run, he failed but with an improved time just outside the threshold. He would have made it if had more time to train. I ran a reasonably good time and came in fifth position.

The Assault Course was a package comprising three clear separate components: a two-mile run in battle order outfit, immediately followed by clearance of the standard obstacle course, and a final run to the live firing range in trench standing position to shoot targets at one hundred metres. As I was the first to arrive at the obstacle course, the first to finish it, and the first to get into the firing trench, I had the most time to rest waiting for nine others to fill the other trenches. My platoon came out tops, and for the effort, we all received a key chain with the SAFTI SSL insignia on the attached medal.

Punishment by my handlers was by meting out 'takes'. A take meant extra duties and could be at Platoon level if meted out by platoon officers or at Section level if meted out by section instructors. These 'takes' included taking on In-Charge (IC) duties that meant more work in having to muster the men, delegate to them specific roles to meet certain demands from on high or to satisfy day-to-day operations and so on. I enjoyed planning and organising, and such extra IC duties were enjoyable. Takes also meant extra guard duties. I truly did not mind these extra guard duties except when they scheduled to the weekends when everyone would joyfully leave camp for home for a reunion with their friends and families. I had the most takes while at the married quarters SAFTI. Whenever I had a reason for doing or not doing something or took the initiative to do something that was useful for the men, they judged them as insubordination. I reckoned it was about following standard operating procedures, regardless of the same or better outcomes. Punishment could be then and there, in a most humiliating fashion that often was testy. Self-restraint necessary to avoid run-ins with handlers, was very much an exercise of humility; the order of the day was compliance and obedience to maintain sanity of the self.

with SSL section mate in drill outfit at SAFTI barracks. The location was the seventh floor of a HDB block of flats among a few others. They called this location 'The Married Quarters' because the blocks of flats fronting the main road housed permanent staff officers and their families. The Married Quarters were about three quarter of a mile to SAFTI camp proper. Most of the training activities and our regular meals happened at SAFTI. You can imagine the number of times we had to move back and forth in a day. I attempted to change things but got into trouble for getting out of line. Trouble meant punishment.

with SSL (School of Section Leaders) section mates in field outfit at SAFTI, either during a break or waiting for some activity to come on. The actual location is at The Married Quarters about three quarter of a mile from SAFTI proper.

5.5 Early NS Disappointment/OCT Interview

Somewhere about the middle of the BMT, we received orders to attend an Officer Cadet screening interview. It was for me a tense moment as I was caught up now between the desire of becoming an officer and a certain disappointment which had turned into a disdain for the military organisation. This disappointment had much to do with the gap between my high expectations of the Armed Forces before my enlistment, and the undesirable reality with which I came face to face in the initial intensive months at it. The gap was significantly wide. I had worked on an unfounded expectation, an ideal that was uneducated and decided upon in isolation of reality. Nevertheless, unbeknown to me at that time I adopted the stance of separation from affiliation with army except for the mandatory requirement to serve.

When I arrived at CMPB (Central Manpower Base), together with others, we ordered and organised ourselves as instructed. As the clerk called out a name, the candidate put on his cap and went into the interview room where the high ranking officers, mostly majors, colonels, and lieutenant colonels convened. Once inside, the candidate stood in the middle as the centre point of a curved panel of tables as though jointed together so that every officer was at an angle directly facing the candidate. The candidate saluted and greeted the panel. When told to sit by the officer in the centre who directly faced him, who appeared to be the chairperson of the panel, he took off the cap and sat on the lone chair provided in the centre of the room, the cap resting on the left lap with its shade pointing to the front. This was standard drill. Were all eyes on him, he could not tell; he was to look straight in the front until addressed by the others to the left or right of the panel, to whom he would then appropriately turn his attention. It might seem intimidating to the reader and in a sense, it was. Yet, as a soldier this was mere duty; there was little tension.

The room was absolutely silent making the place solemn except for the shuffling of papers by the interviewing officers. They appeared drilled as well, taking turns to ask questions. Before the interview, I heard that psychologists were among the interviewers although all wore military uniforms, as though they could read into us. The funny thing was that seated almost unmoved and straight-faced, with no attempts at behavioural 'hoops' I would be surprised they could profile anything unless the candidate was honest and 'angry' as I was. Yet in such circumstances, no one in his sane mind would express his frustrations openly other than a terse 'yes' or 'no'. When the questions allowed room to explain, I had to be cautious and wary of the way I laid my response across to the panel. When the question for me to make a decision to enter Officer Cadet School (OCS) was set forth before me, I simply said I had no interest, and in the event I received assignment to OCS, I would go but not out of any strong desire. Such interviews were a farce as far as my untrained mind could tell. Who can know the heart?

What were the criteria? We hardly knew other than that we have met the requirements for physical and intelligent soundness to lead. These were easy for the interviewers for they needed to look at the test results or reports from our BMT handlers, as well as the pre-enlistment IQ/spatial/personality tests scores. I supposed, that added to these would be someone with a great sense of desire, a loyalty—patriotic sounded a little stretched as we were untested—and integrity, which is also difficult to measure. This was like a grey area that the SAF had failed to gain a handle. In those tests and assessments, I cannot imagine that they could miss an officer's ability to communicate that in turn made command and control manageable. Finally, from a personal viewpoint, one crucial quality missing was common sense; it was so fundamental that it might be difficult to measure. I have seen leaders go through the hoops they have been taught but never getting to the heart of an issue, and therefore unable to seal a perfect closure to it. Perhaps experience shall hone all the weaknesses . . . two and half years were inadequate, so we roll out lesser-baked men.

5.6 Infantry Extension/ Deployment

After the three months of section leaders training at SAFTI, we had learned skills for the parade square as well as in infantry tactics so that we could lead infantrymen in small groups or sections as we called them, to carry out specific tasks to allow other coordinated strategic warfare to proceed and attain its objectives. From basic individual skills in drill, weapon handling, marksmanship, grenade handling, knowledge of support weapons (and we received training on handling the 60 mm mortar bomb), structure of infantry units, disciplinary orders, communications (use of various systems of signalling and codes/call signs, laying communication lines, and the use of radio equipment), command, and control. They called them the 3 C's.

We picked up knowledge in **trench warfare**, making different types of trenches (this was where my construction experience came into good use) of which the stand up bunker trench was toughest. Excavation with changkuls for the big digs was necessary to shorten the time taken to hewn out a trench, refining and packing the sides required a small hand trowel or a short mini changkul that was part of our battle order gear. The height had to fit my height to enable me to have just enough view above, below, and to the sides after packing sandbags just outside the trench level to protect against offensive fire and to allow my rifle to rest when on look outs. For the HQ (headquarters) command trench that was rather large, a mechanical excavator provided the excavation power to quickly dig one out. The exercise was a field operation that lasted several days and took us out to a training ground with a pretty flat mound in Marsiling that we noted as Hill 265. I do not believe it is still there today. Things have changed somewhat with the way military approaches are undertaken today. *It is in discomfort, in the unusual, hemmed-in situations in which one is constrained, and in making the best of it, one learns to cope and become better for it.*

Training over an **obstacle course** required one to be in combat gear with steel helmet, webbing, full water-bottle, rifle, and combat boots. The course began with one getting over a *five foot high concrete wall* about six inches thick. Failure to overcome this first obstacle did not allow a soldier to proceed to the next and very often, we see a congestion of soldiers waiting to try and re-try. I supposed the intention was for it to be the first of several tough stations that paced the course; in short, the first obstacle required much from us in terms of arm strength to pull oneself over and with the legs to assist the climb-over. The next one was a stomach-high *rail barrier* made of steel pipe good for the hand grasp; overall, it was lower and hence easier for one to flip over to the other side. Following this within a few steps was a two and a half feet high *bench* with rolls of barbed wires immediately in front of it to let the soldier experience a mild surprise. One then ran on a ten-inch wide and six feet long wooden plank with steel chains near both ends that kept the plank suspended so that running along it was unstable and tended to sway to off-balance the soldier. There was another similar set-up immediately after this to trouble the soldier who had successfully made past the first. There was no let down in the trial. We called this station, *the short bridge.* Next on the course was the short rope, about eight feet long followed by the high rope probably fifteen feet long, all hanging from A-frames, three ropes to a frame. One had to climb up to the top and touch the metal frame that held the rope. We had been taught the technique of jumping as high as possible to grab the rope to pull oneself up along it with the assistance of the legs to cross-step the rope as leverage, the hands then moved up along it so that the legs repeated the same action until one reached the top. Ropes were easy and required limited arm and leg strength.

One received a slight reprieve as one turned to the right and ran for a short distance to arrive at a series of planks that led up to round logs placed horizontally in *zigzag* fashion. These logs, halved length-wise, so that their diameters were wide enough to fit a single boot step. The soldier had to be precise in the run along the zigzagged logs to finish them without falling off. That was an insidiously precarious obstacle. As one headed down the zigzag, some ten metres in front was a earth-packed *ramp*, a run-up to an eight-foot high retaining wall, from which one had to jump further off to a sand-pit below and avoid the concertina barbed wires that they set up immediately at the bottom of the wall. Several soldiers found the eight feet high jump painful when they ended with hurt ankles from a bad jump. There were a few other obstacles that closely replicated the earlier ones. Right at the end of the course was a singular *long bridge* about ten feet long, much like the earlier two shorter bridges. As soldiers marching to warfare, we will come face to face with obstruction, hindrances, impediments, and things that oppose the way forward, in the physical or moral sense. The obstacle course reminds me of the way life is with its moments of intense difficulty. Sometimes it stretches our stamina, to endure the severe suffering; sometimes our strength, to hold fast at breaking point; at other times, to maintain our balance when meeting the twists and turns that beset us; and still at other times to have the flexibility to manoeuvre through all these demands and come out victorious. *God is our refuge and strength, a very present help in trouble. Therefore will not we fear, though the earth be removed, and though the mountains be carried into the midst of the sea; though the waters thereof roar and be troubled, though the mountains shake with the swelling thereof.*—Psalm 46:1.

The subject of topographical map reading and locating was for all of us commonly known as Topo, short for **topography**. We actually went out to the field to locate spots identified. These spots were not urban buildings and the like. It was more of a unique tree, a stream, a track, a knoll, a deserted hut/shack, a bridge, or a letter box that blended into the terrain and surroundings of a village or cluster of dwellings. As you might now imagine it was really in a countryside setting. Topography was about heights, distances, and directions/orientations—for which a compass was made available to us—between points in places and in objects; it was geography in its breadth and height placed on a flat map and marked out with lines to denote varying heights, a scale to chart the distances, and the longitudinal/latitudinal orientations. Think of Topo as a walk outside of camp and into trees and more trees, into streams, tracks—forked and multi-forked—to test one's ability to accurately locate a position or an object. This was all too familiar, as I had studied topographical map reading in secondary school while studying geography and doing a map survey. Topography with the compass was as a lamp unto our feet and a light unto our path. *Thy word is a lamp unto my feet, and a light unto my path.*—Psalm 119:105.

They channelled some of us into other specialised disciplines. I continued into the infantry, did a short extension that they called a conversion course, after which we were posted to other units to instruct new intakes of recruits entering the BMT or to take up operational duties.

The Hokkien Platoon of Kranji Camp out on field
exercise. I was not in the picture

National Service had been for me a priceless time capsule. It captured all shades of human experience cast in the form of discipline and laze, of fear and courage, of aggression and condescension, of taking and giving orders, of risk and caution, of integrity and compromise, of strength and weakness, of mind and matter, of patriotic loyalty simmered in rebellion. It was a time when restlessness rankled with anger and drew very clear lines that marked themselves deeply and distinctly in the sands of the time and age. It was . . . to secure the truth . . . tearing through the tapestry of tradition and expectations to pursue truth about life. It was in that most destructive of moments that a new peace arrived . . . Restlessness reached its peak towards the end of National Service.

5.7 Operational Hokkien Company

My Hokkien Company of men was an unhappy lot who hated National Service even though they had two years to serve while we the more educated had a two and a half years stint. They came away from their private working lives to mandatorily enlist in this poorly paid constrained service where occasional reprieves (booking out) on weekends and secret gambling sessions provided the only release from their frustrations.

Burt and several others were formerly boatmen from another infantry unit. Burt's brother died in one of their exercises and this hung over their outlooks. Generally, he and those with him looked dimly on National Service but they were the morose and more sensible lot than the rest in the platoon. The difficult experience they went through seemed to have touched a strain in their hearts perhaps thankful of having survived where others had not made it. Burt was an important and significant ally for one as me who was raw, inexperienced, one who knew little beyond books and poverty, one who was of few words. Physically he was a hulk; at heart, he was sensible and you could reason with him. On moral principles, I stood very tall, would never budge or flinch, and his common sense and reason bought into me as his trusted, fair and equitable handler. There was not so much about the wisdom; it was truly and simply the application of clear definite principles. Looking back, I realised the folly, in a sense, in my approach but once again our Lord God Almighty in His providence had given me another gang leader to watch out for me in possible conflicts; that in itself was a deterrent to offence. *By me princes rule, and nobles, even all the judges of the earth.*—Proverbs 8:16.

Many of the men in the Hokkien platoon, taken out of their personal freedom and regular better paid work as tradesmen, contractors, and so on, to serve two years in National Service felt a sense of income lost, of time wasted and lost opportunities. Pay or wages at ninety dollars a month during National Service was a paltry token, a pittance.

Others felt their lifestyles curtailed such as Tiger Cub. My encounters with him were truly enriching for me. He was a reckless loud mouthed gang leader, medium built, a smoker, likes to go bare top to show off his Tiger Cub tattoos. He had a right hand man named Water who balanced out all of Tiger Cub's extremities and kept up the sanity of the gang. There was an occasion when I had to get Tiger Cub out of his bed on the upper deck of the double-decker bed, so that he was like everyone else without the special privileges his gang had showered on him. First move was to command by shouting into his ears where he had pulled the blanket over his face. He became irritated, sat up immediately to challenge me, and threatened with taking me on over the weekend outside of camp. That meant an invitation to a fight. My response was for us to sort out the matter there and then; no deferment to the weekend was necessary. He jumped out of bed and was almost ready to take me on, while for me it was a brave gamble. Water was ever faithful and rushed to separate us. With wisdom, Water persuaded Tiger Cub against a showdown. We got on with the work at hand. My gamble was that he could not take me on in the barracks where military law prevailed; outside camp, the law of the jungle could prevail. If it had headed for a showdown then, I had enough faith that Burt and his gang would likely lend support. Of course, this was never tested.

'Water' was also a promoter for Tiger Cub, ran errands that benefited Tiger Cub such as whisking him off 5BX (five basic exercises) at dawn when shadows made for easy dark transactions. I was always there to spot the stealthy moves and put Tiger Cub back where he rightly belonged. He had no love for my hounding him; he had some respect for my sharp wit in anticipating his next step. I was never quite able to understand all such behaviours, suspecting that the harder times they went through in the boat company had bonded these men as brothers, each watching out for the other, balancing out each other's extremities or weaknesses. Such was the camaraderie among them.

Still others did not really care too much about their stints in National Service. They simply wanted an easy time, served the mandatory term, and be returned to the real world or the 'civvy' (meaning civilian) life. Ong was from the seamier side of town and lived in the red light Desker Road area. I could see that he knew a lot about people in those quarters and sensed he consistently restrained himself from saying too much. My sense was that he did not wish to present himself a pimp in everyone's eyes, of which I never ever knew that he was one in spite of the few hints he laid on from time to time. Ong acted silly, and spoke in a low slow drawl that with all ranks of people, he was forgivable as dim-witted. Among platoon mates, Ong was the platoon lookout man while the others gambled behind cupboards. He ironed uniforms for fifty cents apiece while acting as lookout. He would shout out loudly "Sir" on the pretext of acknowledging an officer's approach to the platoon's bunks. That would put the gamblers behind the cupboards on alert to end whatever they were doing, to get off their beds, tidy up, and in 'ready' mode. A year or two later after ROD, I bumped into Ong in the Collyer Quay area and he was working as a bank despatch clerk. In my eyes, he was a natural survivor, low key with very little known about him, evasive somewhat, no known convictions of any sort and bent with the wind, or disappear to blend into the massing crowd. If he ever stood out, it was to exhibit his ineptness; when in trouble he faded quietly as one no different from the crowd. I always thought he made a good spy.

Internal Security (IS). The IS drill was short, sharp, and unconventional that would take opponents by surprise. It was no longer just marching in standard formation. We had quick time marching like halving the regular march speed, a sort of quick time, and double quick time with the boots hitting hard and sharp, so that the sense of urgency was there, an aura of tenseness filled the air, and our hearts and minds on high alert. We used forty-five degree turns that could easily surprise a riotous crowd and when we quick-marched in that formation, with rifles at half-port, with gas masks installed, I could imagine the fear that the formation imposed on any rowdy assembly. We employed shouts to rouse fear and exuded an unrestrained readiness to squash any uprising. It all made for a sharp and sleek force that reeked of a robotic, cold, and unemotional approach to dealing with violence: forceful wrath for wilful rebellion.

As part of the Internal Security drills, we underwent training to experience tear gas and understand its employment in times of internal security violations. The gas was quite biting and painful. For the first time in my life, I realised the tear gas had a fearsome effect on our soldiers. Fear in man heightened when we put them with gas masks in pitch dark underground mazes of tunnels with plenty of tear gas thrown into them. Not many survived the ordeal. Tough and loud talking men in the broad daylight when subjected to the darkness and the unknown, fell victim to fear and lose their minds to let go of the webbing of the man in front of him to attempt to 'save' himself and in the course lose the 'lifeline', and was lost in the tunnel. When the gas started to bite their skins and cause irritation and hurt, these men struggled against their own masks and pulled them off in panic and fear. Without the man in front of him at the beginning, he was lost, disoriented, and eventually overwhelmed by the absence of an anchor. That worsened their condition, and when he pulled off the gas mask in panic, he lost all sense of orientation, and slid into the gripping fear of death eventually, only for another to remove from and dragged out of the tunnels by force. This presented a sharp contrast to who he was under normal circumstances. I led seven men into the tunnels, and only two came out with me. The five who failed to exit from the tunnels, were necessarily lost and had to be rescued; they came out with uncontrollable tears from the effects of the gas, their faces all red from irritation and pain caused by the gas. Tiger Cub was among the five. They were like babies crying out loud, gasping for air, and vomited. It was a humbling exercise for us all. The tear gas saved their embarrassment. I had never understood the tear gas and its effects. What I saw on television were those in the news about disturbances in foreign countries where tear gas canisters thrown by law enforcers at rioting crowds in broad daylight and in open spaces to turn them away. Having experienced its effects on the human body exposed to it, there was a little more respect for tear gas. It was something we learned not to take lightly. I had also the rare and unusual opportunity to use a gas mask and understand its workings. The closed and pitch dark maze of tunnels filled with much tear gas offered us an extreme experience that truly brought out its efficacy to ward off and deter crowds. More importantly, it revealed the response of an untrained person and the human reactions to the unknown. This episode was inerasable from my life experiences; its imprint was priceless. I was sure that when the men had to do it again, they would come out better. Experience was often a good teacher.

There was at a time some years earlier, that a terrorist hijack of a ship off our waters that Operations T was born. From then on, operational units such as ours took up stations to **protect major installations** as oil refineries of BP (British Petroleum) at Labrador, Esso at Pulau Ayer Chawan, Shell at Pulau Merlimau, power stations at Jurong and Pasir Panjang. These were 'live' operations where we protected the sites on a week-long cycle and returned to camp for our regular activities. Other platoons or companies took over and the rotation went on. Often when I looked back at this and other activities we undertook during the operational days, I realised that when in uniform, there was this huge sense of duty, not patriotism or anything. I remembered the heightened level of vigilance I adopted that I transferred to the men under my charge. They were much unimpressed; it was for them "as normal, take it easy man, don't be so serious . . ." Position implies responsibility. *Our attitudes play a big part in all that we do. National Service and all the little things in it, was for me a big thing.*

During field exercises, moving as a platoon in the several sections, there were times we helped with support arms. The 60 mm mortar was memorable in that it was rather heavy and when dismantled provided the component parts: the barrel, the base plate that was the heaviest part and the clumsiest to carry, the legs, and the elevation sight set. The saving grace was having a leather strap to hold the base plate to hang it over one's body. Several of us took turns to carry the base plate travelling across long distances over hilly terrain, climbing over mounds, and finally positioning the mortar in mock battle, and moving on again.

Field camp was all about camping out in the training grounds at Tekong where for a week we saw only forests and trees, some hilly spots, and all things of nature. It was about raising bashas (tents) to provide shelter from the cold and rain amidst the trees. One got wet when the rain was heavy, the thin tent material leaked; it was less than waterproof. Eating from the aluminium mess cans saw our food filled with rain water. We dug deep holes in the ground to simulate toilet holes, and for sanitation, with chemical powder sprinkled into the human excreta after the user had completed his purges. The chemical was to detoxify the faeces and also kept away the flies. For limited privacy, a roll of Hessian sheet of two feet in width wrapped around several iron pickets to define small squat-height private 'cubicles'. During breaks in the late afternoons when training was lighter, the CSM (company sergeant major who was a WO or warrant officer) an ex-commando showed off his skills using his special commando hand knife to remove a large centipede's fangs and then letting it crawl all over him. Such were the times where there was a lot of show-off in a man's world, with talk of past glories unknown to anyone else, etc. We received lessons on how to slaughter chickens when in the field, eating insects, and so on. Of course, it was all theory with nothing practical to show. In time of war, I might just string a dozen of them together in a strait-jacketed box and put a single bullet through their bodies. Again, that is another theory.

Our company commander, a captain in rank, was a regular officer (permanent staff); the second in command (2IC) was a National Service young Indian lawyer; the platoon commander was also an Indian lawyer on National Service. The alternate Company 2IC was an Arab from RI (Raffles Institution) known for his long distance running prowess would regularly take the men out at the end of a rough day through tough physical exercises and strenuous runs along the sharply undulating tracks of the armoured centre's ammunition dump. These were tracks used by armoured vehicles and tanks, difficult and meant for those war machines. Trying to make men run on these tracks was seriously a little less than human. Treating men as though they were machines and subjecting them to the rigours constructed for machines deserve a snub. When men were under authority, there was little to murmur against. The worst kind of treatment was when we returned from a long field march in battle order and received punishment in the form of fifty push-ups due to some murmuring and non-cooperation from some men. With heavy gear, boots heavy with mud, legs all limp, arms with no traction, bodies burdened, and breaths withering, the fifty push-ups were simply a call for mutiny. Of course, in the military at platoon level in peace time, mutiny in the camp had the least probability with all the attendant risks of punishment, detention, and extension of the ROD (run-out-date). There was no more than a great deal of whining and disgruntlement, quickly forgotten the next day.

On another occasion, I had a run-in with the company quartermaster (CQ) who at one time called out 'corporal' with my back facing him. I did not respond, as he did not address my name. Other 'corporals' were also present at that time. He imagined that I had been insubordinate to him who was a regular (permanent) staff as I walked off from the scene. From then on, I was a marked man and he seized every available opportunity to inflict pain on me. There was once when an immediate mustering of the men was called for and everyone slipped on the army issued canvas shoes, or slippers, in T-shirts of red or green etc like a rag-tag band of men, some of whom were in the shower, some resting, others in an activity of some kind. It was for some announcements by the company Second-In-Command (2IC). I slipped on my personal black canvas shoes with the heel folded down simulating a slipper; these were not the regular army issued ones. The CQ spotted that and after the announcements, insisted I reported to the 2IC's office. He charged me for misuse of army property. I refuted the charge and let the 2IC know it was my personal pair and I wore it as a slip-on rather than a wear-on at that time under the immediate falling circumstance. The 2IC did not charge me but offered me two takes' meaning two punishments of extra duties. The 2IC was being diplomatic to not offend the CQ, and in the pecking order, I was due to take the rap. It was nothing new; I had taken all the extras at SAFTI. When under NS, rank and law, military law, mattered. You cannot quit a mandatory service as you can in civilian law. There was a pecking order. We can stand up for what is right and be ready to face possible adverse consequences.

Punishment in an operational unit appeared as a thing more seriously applied than in training units; I supposed it had to do with an expectation of discipline, as well as the kind of people we had to put up with. In such a unit of rough grained men who sought every opportunity to conduct themselves violently, settling differences mostly outside of camp on the weekends soon after they booked out was a common thing. In one case, appointed together with another NCO we escorted the handcuffed accused before the Disciplinary Officer to mete out a disciplinary order for beating up an NCO outside of camp. The drill was again in quick time, the air filled with expectancy of an escape or of violence about to occur. That put the escort NCOs on a particularly high alert and the accused in a state of facing verbal abuse/intimidation and judgement. It was unlike in a civil hearing but one where there was a great deal of shouting with intimidation in mind to secure a 'guilty' plea and summarily passing the attendant judgement. The punishment would be restraint or detention at the guard house for weeks or months depending on the severity of the offence. At times that meant also an extension of the accused's National Service stint by the term of detention. The whole disciplinary process was a sort of mini court martial.

There was a general call-up for pre-university NCOs (non-commissioned officers) to attend an OCT interview outside of Kranji Camp at the Central Manpower Base (CMPB), generally a welcomed trip to the city. Half a dozen of us herded on to a three-tonner military truck that would take us there. When it stopped at the main entrance to get clearance, I jumped off and made the slip. OCT interviews were for me pointless; I have made a clear stand against it months ago when I had my first one. Interestingly enough, there were no reprisals; the matter never came up for comment.

Two and a half years in National Service had been for me a priceless time capsule. They captured all shades of human experience cast in the form of discipline and laze, of fear and courage, of aggression and condescension, of taking and giving orders, of risk and caution, of integrity and compromise, of strength and weakness, of mind and matter, of patriotic loyalty simmered in rebellion. It was a time when restlessness rankled with anger and drew very clear lines that marked themselves deeply and distinctly in the sands of the time and age. It was as going for a punch out with restlessness to secure the truth, going for broke tearing through the tapestry of tradition and expectations to pursue truth about life. It was in that most destructive of moments that a new peace arrived when it all became clear what the purpose of life was. Restlessness reached its peak towards the end of National Service. It was a time when most things seemed to be hopelessly out of alignment or synchrony with what should be, it was a time one wished to right all that was wrong, yet there were too many wrongs to right. It was not to be one man's calling but merely a passing beckon to which no response was required. More importantly, we knew we would break out of that time capsule to enter the real world with which we were uncertain could be better.

With fellow officers of the Hokkien Platoon at the then only ice skating rink in Taman Jurong. I was on photo's far right.

Now restlessness mingled with malaise. It was a truly empty shell of a life, filled with activities that made no sense and yet was a pleasant break. There was a lingering void, a languid listless unhappily inexpressible time. Indifference seemed to have overwhelmed me; I was spiritless.

6.

At Twenty—Wasting Away; Uncertain World Ahead

For if the trumpet give an uncertain sound,
who shall prepare himself to the battle?
—1 Corinthians 14:8.

A t the age of twenty, I was moved to the Third Brigade Band and within the first week, I fell ill. I ran a high fever and was completely ill at ease. This new posting was totally 'impossible' for me. Discipline in military terms was weak. Life was very sedentary; there were no drills, no running, no carrying of rifles, no shouting, no tension, and . . . just nothing. My body simply could not handle this. My body died and I had a serious visit to the Medical Centre. I had never reported sick since entering National Service and this was my first. It was so bad the medical officer gave me a jab while lying helpless on my back on a flat surface. It knocked me unconscious. When I awoke, still on my back, I could see the ceiling fan whirling over me, as though the helicopter was taking me away to safety as in a war zone. It took a few more minutes to overcome the nausea, letting blood find all the channels in the brain to restore life, and soon a feeling of reality returned as in coming back from the dark absence.

The return to the band started poorly in its routine of ease and lack of sharpness that contrasted the routine of intense physical discipline forced and expected in infantry training. To bridge the difficulty I initiated running round the field at the end of the day to allow me to take out the slack. This progressed into soccer matches among the members. Not all members participated in the sport as we had a rather lazy democracy at the band. We mandated that everyone played soccer, those who did not had to run around the field at least three rounds. Usually soccer time outlasted the three rounds of running and those folks when they had finished, went on to rest, shower, and prepare to book out of camp when it was time to do so. Eventually soccer became more serious and we began competing with teams outside of camp.

The 3rd Brigade Band's barracks at Gothic Line in
Portsdown Camp. I was first on the photo's left.

6.1 Posting to the 3rd Brigade Band

When informed of my posting to the Third Brigade Band while at the height of operational activity surprise overtook me. It was unimaginable, inconceivable. It must have been a mistake as reality settled in. I checked it out and found out those instructions came from Mindef. I had a few days to pack up, and I duly checked out of Kranji Camp after a brief meeting with the company commander to officially despatch me.

A land rover picked me up and despatched me to the Third Brigade Band. It was back to a familiar place in the Portsdown Camp or Slim Barracks. When serving out BMT, I was at the El Alamein block, this time it was the Gothic Line, two blocks away. I reported to the office and met the company sergeant major (CSM) who was Indian, and a Warrant Officer in rank. He had been in the SAF a really long time. I could sense his certain disdain for 'A' levels NS men. I was not of many words and asked the most important question: "Why was I posted to the Third Brigade Band." He explained that they were short-handed with a declining cohort of retiring regulars/permanent staff. Recruiting experienced regulars was difficult and hence they resorted to enlisting NS men with previous band experience. That sounded like a very sensible move. After going through the papers, he had me waiting to meet the Director of Music (DOM), a Malay Captain. The meeting with the DOM went smoothly and he enquired the instrument I last played, which was the trumpet. He wanted to know what other instruments I could play proficiently at, which was the euphonium/baritone, the G-horn, and bass. The cornet assigned to me was the standard instrument used instead of the trumpet when playing in concert. The DOM, known as an excellent trumpeter was nicknamed Singapore's Harry King after the famous deceased trumpeter in the U.S. He went to the Royal School of Music (RSM) in England to study music and band leadership. The DOM could transliterate music and edit scores. The CSM ran the band in its day to day matters since the DOM's primary role was in the musical side of things. Understanding the organisation was important as I considered a band to run quite differently from an operational infantry unit. Yet there must be the necessary discipline especially when the band often became an important component of a march past, in a parade, at the Istana's monthly Changing of the Guards or at the Istana grounds to receive credentials of new incoming foreign ambassadorial appointees.

My second day at the band was engaged in observation of the typical daily band activities. There was area cleaning and muster parade in the morning, followed by instrumental group practices, and a combined practice at an hour before noon to go through music scores in preparation for a public appearance at the Botanic Gardens or at the National Theatre or at an Istana Dinner for a special occasion, and so on. The schedules were seldom hectic and were well spaced out. Life was at a leisurely pace.

I was in the course of my time at the band, exposed to new well known trumpet personalities that highlighted the many possibilities in jazz music and I was very much excited about it. "Doc" Severinsen was an American pop and jazz trumpeter best known for leading the NBC Orchestra on *The Tonight Show Starring Johnny Carson*. I learned about Doc at a music record shop during one of my time-off days from the band. Browsing for trumpet musicians in the jazz category, I saw that the shop had carried many of his recordings. I tried several and liked his music. I did not have a record player and requested for the shop to copy them on to audio cassette tapes that I then collected on another day. In those days, audio CDs were not in existence. Audio cassettes were by far cheaper than buying music scores. I spent much listening and trying to write down in skeletal musical form that allowed to play from memory or *ad lib* somewhat. This was still feasible as our preoccupation was music with very few serious duties to attend.

Miles Davis was an American jazz musician, trumpeter, bandleader, and composer. Widely considered one of the most influential musicians of the 20th century, Miles Davis was, with his musical groups, at the forefront of several major developments in jazz music, including bebop and jazz fusion. I did not particularly like fusion jazz, preferring the traditional form. Bebop was not even under my music radar. I did not truly delve into Davis' work, as there was little availability of materials featuring him. Singapore was supposedly some years behind the United States in the jazz music scene. Big band music was more popular at that time than jazz.

At the Istana grounds. I was second from photo's left with
hands un-gloved and held together in front.

At a parade march past. I was the first on the photo's left in the foreground, playing the cornet, the band's standard issue. Its tone is rounder and mellower.

At the front of the then National Theatre. I was
in back row, third from photo's left.

6.2 From the Rough to the Slack

Over the next few days without the tough physical activity of an operational infantry unit, I was completely uneasy. It was as though physical activity was a drug infusion without which the body could not function properly. On the second day, I was unable to cope with the lack of serious activity. I felt chilly and by the afternoon was running a low fever. I fought it for a while, asked the clerk for Paracetamol (Panadol was the brand) to stay what I thought was a temporary indisposition. The next morning I ran quite a fever and took off to the Medical Centre. Waiting for the Medical Officer took a long while; I struggled to maintain clarity and alertness that was rapidly declining. Finally, the Medical Officer arrived, asked a few questions, looked at the notes taken by the Medical Orderly, and asked for the needle and a tiny vial of clear liquid into which he pushed the needle to draw out the liquid. He pushed it into my upper arm muscle and I felt very queasy completely unable to fight off the overwhelming torpor that had hit like a rock. I saw the overhead ceiling fan whirling at top speed and felt the wind attempting to remove the heat of my body. I knocked out completely, insensible, not remembering a thing when I woke up which must have been some hours. The nausea was still there; I was completely weak and wanted to simply lie there for as long as I could. This experience of separating from my own consciousness was frightening and was my first. It was an uncanny entry to my days at the band.

6.3 Getting Used to Laze and Boredom

That first week at the third brigade band was quite an experience. The second week was no better; the pace of work was a crawl, too leisurely for my liking. The workload was not meaningful. Not everyone was bothered about excellence; many have gotten accustomed to doing just enough and enjoying the ease. By then, I felt the urge to go for a run around the field after the company dismissed the men and everyone could book out of camp. I did this for a few days and suggested to the CSM to spruce the men up by having the hour before book-out for physical activities. He agreed to the suggestion and as expected there was an outcry and so we added soccer to it. This was a good move, the interest level went up, and soon we had a team of reasonably good players and trained together. We arranged soccer competition outside of camp on weekends. I became more alive; some colours added to my outlook, life at band became more enjoyable.

6.4 Lingering Void

Among other things that changed at the band was that the cohort of NS men found a fellowship among themselves. We all had a term to serve and it would run out months apart from each other. Our ages were about a year apart; the interests were relatively similar. We visited music stores, went to SAF Enterprises clubhouse to swim when we had time-off from having to attend a changing of guards at the Istana or providing music at a public place on weekends. We went fishing, hiking, and the like. There was a great deal of freedom to pursue our interests and yet the tough and tumble of the year earlier in the infantry had taken out my interest in many things I used to be interested in. Now restlessness mingled with malaise. It was a truly empty shell of a life, filled with activities that made no sense and yet was a pleasant break. There was a lingering void, a languid listless unhappily inexpressible time. Indifference seemed to have overwhelmed me; I was spiritless.

6.5 Religion in certain Declension

My belief in Buddhism had declined into the abyss of meaninglessness. There was no turning back in my total disbelief in nirvana, so central to and fundamental in Buddhism. The search continued and ran into dangerous domains as I read about and dabbled in the mystic and spiritual matters, even experimented in the Ouija board with camp mates. My conclusion was that they did nothing more than satisfy my curiosity but took me nowhere. They could not satisfy my hungering cry for knowledge of my existence, the purpose of life, and ultimate meaning for an existence. Going to the temple became a mere weekly ritual that did not excite me one jot. There were times I would skip it altogether on some pretext. It was truly a suffering to still be in 'no man's land'. How could I go on to live a life, do the things I want to do, pursue goals, and the like when directionless in the spirit? I can pretend to just do it, to do what was expected, and just get on in life. I truly needed help that I simply could not fathom from whence it would come.

6.6 Draw Nigh unto Him, He Will Draw Nigh . . . I was found!

We have all been wayward; we have all gone astray, in that we look to the world to satisfy our deep-seated hunger and thirst for God. We must acknowledge our transgression when we rejected Him in the first instance. It must not be taken lightly when we reflect how blatantly we cast Him aside in all our worldly deliberations, how we mocked at Him, bashed His followers, humiliate them, and treated them scornfully for no other reason than that they believed in Christ while we believed not. God has left us with a mind for Him yet we wilfully reject Him. He so loved the world. We must turn from our waywardness and draw near to Him. We have reconciliation when we believe in His plan of grace and have faith that Jesus Christ, the only begotten Son of God died on the cross at Calvary so that we should not perish but have everlasting life.

For God so loved the world, that he gave his only begotten Son, that whosoever believeth in him should not perish, but have everlasting life.—John 3:16.

Submit yourselves therefore to God. Resist the devil, and he will flee from you.—James 4:7.

Draw nigh to God, and he will draw nigh to you. Cleanse your hands, ye sinners; and purify your hearts, ye double minded.—James 4:8.

Humble yourselves in the sight of the Lord, and he shall lift you up.—James 4:10.

For the law made nothing perfect, but the bringing in of a better hope did; by the which we draw nigh unto God.—Hebrews 7:19.

When in desperation in my search for meaning, when it was truly a search for God, one that I was too proud to admit, I turned to the Gospels of the Bible. There I found Jesus speaking to me directly ready to teach me the truth as I open my heart and mind to Him. As He spoke in the inspired gospels, I saw His goodness and mercy. He was the way, the truth, and the light. *Jesus saith unto him, I am the way, the truth, and the life: no man cometh unto the Father, but by me. If ye had known me, ye should have known my Father also: and from henceforth ye know him, and have seen him.*—John 14:6-7.

6.7 ROD

This was a sweet name for most of us while still in National Service. ROD stood for 'Run-Out-Date', the day we had all been waiting for. It was as though the two and half years uprooted from our individual timelines, shifted to National Service in a time cell, and now having served its time, and officially released from it. It was a day when one discharged from a mandatory two and a half years detention or confinement term, free once again to enter society. Today, we call it ORD (Operationally Ready Date).

ROD was something of a talking point while in National Service. If one met another new colleague the first questions would be where one came from, the last unit or camp, then ROD would pop up next; it was a gauge of when one joined and when one would be getting out and hence how long more one had to serve. Nothing mattered more than getting out. This was much like in prison where inmates talk about how long they have been in and when they would get out. There was a sense of notching up experiences in the time served and yet looking forward to the discharge from 'constraint', from confinement. The question of 'why' one was in there may be answered in a terse 'theft', 'pushing drugs', 'vandalism', 'rape', 'consuming drugs', 'CBT' . . . and so on. In National Service, no one ever asked 'why' one was in it; all able-bodied young men who reached that age came as assigned and resigned to it. Very naturally, National Service had become an event where one did not have a choice, it was an event where one went away from society to train and develop as soldiers in preparation for an unknown possible war or disturbance in the future that could also not happen at all. To have is better than to risk not having. The cost conceivably was calculated to be worthy of having National Service.

ROD had then a connotation of going through and ending something of a chore, drudgery; something unpleasant with everyone waiting to abort when time reaches its full season. Today's ORD most certainly mean the date when a soldier becomes operationally ready to undertake duties for which he trained. Times have changed, the Hokkien Company who spoke only dialect, do not now exist to bear an understanding of ROD or ORD in English or any of their nuances.

ROD: an outing with fellow 3rd Brigade bandsmen at
Pulau Ubin. I was 4th from the photo's right

ROD: another shot of the Pulau Ubin outing. I was seated on right.

Before ROD: a day out fishing in open waters . . . I caught nothing

6.8 Turning Twenty One

National Service, by design seemed like a time when one trained and developed as soldiers, yet also a time to take one into adulthood. In a universal sense, age twenty one is the time when one receives the 'key' to independence, traditionally and legally. In a sense, National Service prepared one for manhood. It was in this latter sense that National Service was meaningful to me, not so much of the age.

Twenty one meant I accepted manhood. I must go it alone. I must make the major decisions of life. I no longer rely and lean on traditions, or on others, to whom I conventionally go for direction. I was to have my own mind in decisions; I can and must still seek counsel.

At home, Mie bought a cake in the shape of a key to celebrate my twenty first birthday. Mie also cooked a simple meal including a bowl of a substitute longevity noodles with slices of liver and a half-boiled egg. I had my family and my nieces around for company; it was as though I have moved on. Simple . . . a celebration without any great joy, as an initiation into possible excitement or gloom and no one knew. There was significance to mildly put it, for to Mie, it was not just an event to mark that coming of age, but particularly meaningful and a 'must-have' for the oldest boy in the family. With little else done for me, I prepared to work it through on my own in the years ahead. It was as in the American Indian story that when one came of age, one was sent out into the wilderness with the tomahawk, the bow and arrows, a knife, and moccasins—the essentials for survival. I was thankful for my 'premier' education, for a supportive and encouraging home environment, and a knowledge that God exists. That God will rule in my life from henceforth was the most critical one. I will soon have to tell the world including my parents. There were unknown consequences to face. My zeal for Christ was deep and strong that I would follow Him where he beckons. Those were my essentials. It was clear that I was to go out there in the 'wilderness' and work with all the circumstances that would befall me on the journey of life.

My humble 21st Birthday Celebration with family

For all the time that I have intentionally and knowingly ignored God, shut Him out of my mind and my heart, avoided Him at all cost, shuttered my eyes to His Word, stopped my ears from His living voice; in His love He worked on me, He bided His time. I ran from Him, I fled from His presence, hid from His truth, mocked His Word, derided His followers, marked an atheist, and a known anti-Christ among friends. In His goodness and mercy, in His abounding Grace He gently tarried, and when I have exhausted all the doors I could knock on, I peeked into His open inviting door . . .

7.

Meeting Jesus

One adequate support
For the calamities of mortal life
Exists; one only—an assured belief
That the procession of our fate, howe'er
Sad or disturbed, is ordered by a
Being of infinite benevolence and power,
Whose everlasting purposes embrace
All accidents, converting them to good.
—William Wordsworth

When I first met Jesus in the Four Gospels according to (written by) four different writers (Matthew, Mark, Luke, and John) addressed to different audiences depicting Jesus as King, Servant, Son of man, and Son of God, I found in Christ the same Person consistent in all that He said, thought, and did. He was the Person I had been looking for in as many years that I was a Buddhist where no immaculately perfect, almighty, omniscient, omnipresent persona existed. Jesus showed me who He was, is, and forever be, immutable and eternal. Jesus revealed He is the Son of God and God at the same time.

Much of his youthful life was not recorded but where it was reported in the gospel, he was consistently in his heavenly Father's will: *and . . . grew, and waxed strong in spirit, filled with wisdom: and the grace of God was upon him . . . . when he was twelve years old, they went up to Jerusalem . . . they found him in the temple, sitting in the midst of doctors, both hearing them, and asking questions. And all that heard him were astonished at his understanding and answers . . . And Jesus increased in wisdom and stature, and in favour with God and man.*—Luke 2:40-51. He was without blemish, faultless. His teaching throughout was absolute and without compromise. There was no instance His doctrine changed relative to new circumstances. *And they were astonished at his doctrine: for his word was with power.*—Luke 4:32. No man ever did what He did; no man ever spoke as He spoke. He never exhibited showiness of character; he did not come across as one who lusted after power, or as someone who sought fame and fortune. As a carpenter he was of a lowly occupation; his station in life was obscure. He came out of an unknown place of Nazareth such that one of his future disciples asked, *"Can there any good thing come out of Nazareth?"*—John 1:46. His ambition was not to be like the world but with a single-mindedness to do as His Father willed. Yet, his influence extended far and wide, deep and high. He exuded compassion in all his dealings. He struck me as someone with complete authority over all the elements; He was able to hold them together, employ them, and deploy them with ease, to cast His own inherent perfection subject to His Father's will, in an integrated coherence that was way beyond my imagination and comprehension. He had perfect poise. *And they were all amazed, and spake among themselves, saying, what a word is this! For with authority and power he commandeth the unclean spirits, and they come out. And the fame of him went out into every place of the country round about.*—Luke 4:36-37. I threw all of myself at His feet all prepared to recognise Him as Master, Teacher, and Lord over my life. He was completely overwhelming; absolutely and unreservedly, His righteousness, His wisdom, His love, His completeness, His utter Perfection overcame me. He was the Forever Absolute, the Eternal One. In the four gospels, there was simply no evidence that He was inconsistent, there was no instance He could not solve a problem and when He did, it was perfectly congruent with His nature, in His righteousness, and in His holiness. It was little wonder that Jesus was known by names such as the Master, Physician, Teacher, 'One Come from God', Rabbi, Lamb of God, King, and Lord.

He was no populist, no men pleaser. He came not to destroy that which God had of old instituted but to fulfil it. There was not one like Him in all my readings: not one statesman be it Churchill, Gandhi, Kennedy, Nixon or our own Prime Minister then; not one conqueror, ruler, or leader be it Nebuchadnezzar, Alexander the Great, Darius, Caesar, Napoleon, Genghiz Khan, MacArthur or Rommel; not one world renowned teacher be it Aristotle, Socrates, Buddha, Confucius or Laotzu, or Kant. Not one single soul dead or alive came anywhere close to who Jesus was and what He did. Jesus was incomparable in that He stood alone in greatness. Jesus exhibited no sophistication of great men of the world, yet his majesty rose above and beyond the reach of all. In all the height of His stature, Jesus spoke to the heart of the ordinary child, man, and woman.

Not for a moment did I think of anything or anyone else. Christ so captivated my thought, excited my search for one such as He that I wanted to read through those four gospels again and again to satisfy myself that I was not reading into them. They were revealing the truth, the way, and the life to my lost soul buffeted by the numerous unanswered foundational questions in the many years I have lived. I read through the gospels two more times, and at the end of it, in my bed, amidst opposing voices, I spoke to Him and thanked Him for the revelation of Himself to me. Those opposing voices attempted to veer me away from setting aside Buddhism by unfolding the challenges I would face before Pa, and everyone else; the loss of many commendations and status worked and accumulated over the years. They were futile, for in Jesus I had found my adoration. *And such as do wickedly against the covenant shall he corrupt by flatteries: but the people that do know their God shall be strong, and do exploits.*—Daniel 11:32.

All that I have read about Him in the gospels easily overwhelmed me to convince of His deity. I am His and will always be His, at His beck and call, doing His will. I knew what I meant. I still had no deeper understanding than that Jesus was all that mattered to me. There were heights of His walk as man and depths in His Being, and in His Death on the cross that I could not fathom fully at that time. I was at the surface and yet His Godliness manifested with such peace and rest in my soul that He was the One I have always sought. There was so much still to know about Jesus that this human lifetime may not afford. It mattered little except that I should commit myself and follow the tug of my heart. He was captivating. He set me the captive, free from the bondage of doubt about the meaning of life. Yet, He captivated me, all of me; I was a liberated captive from darkness, all ready to be a captive in Christ's light. *The Spirit of the Lord GOD is upon me; because the LORD hath anointed me to preach good tidings unto the meek; he hath sent me to bind up the broken hearted, to proclaim liberty to the captives, and the opening of the prison to them that are bound.*—Isaiah 61:1

This whole episode of my 'turning and tossing' was over a period of three days and two nights of reading the four gospels, re-reading, thinking, and in buffetings that opposed my embrace of Jesus. There was no rest during those moments. There was no way I would run away from Him. He was too excellent a Person in all that He said and did in the gospels. I wanted to know what He looked like yet in all His excellences my human conception of an image of Christ was clearly impossible to conjure or define. He was more than mortal man, that in the limitations and nature of mortal man can he ever be humanly portrayed? One's knowledge of Christ cannot adequately be painted and set on a canvas. Knowledge paints the portrait of Jesus in our character. He had about Him an indescribable incommunicable grandeur and brilliance that stood Him out in all of history. He was peerless . . . He was truly God.

My whole being turned about, my mind ready to conform to His way of thinking, and ready to deploy at His command. A pre-occupation with Jesus in all that He presented before me in the gospels made sleep to be of no consequence; just engrossed in thinking about Him was the sustaining strength. I thanked God that He provided the time when my two and a half years of National Service was nearing the end and the duties tended to lighten, with the clearance of our annual leave (vacation) entitlement almost a common practice. My readers do well to note that physically I was the same person, the same mortal man of flesh and blood as I was before I met Jesus; what changed was my mind that desired an alignment to His way of thinking, my heart to be able to feel like His, so very deeply thoughtful. My cup emptied out and sought only His filling, I simply thirsted for the Christ I had read about, seen, and heard in the gospels. I thirsted for life, the Life that only He could give. I wanted an infusion of His character, of His nature, His incomparable wisdom, the coherence, and perfection in His great work in setting men free from the bondage of sin and all its darkness. He had a perfect knowledge of man, of man's nature, of man's thoughts, and its workings that brought forth from Him the most precise replies to man's inner thoughts and questions. He saw the depths of our soul and in a word, tore through to the centre of man's being. It reminds me of Peter's denial of Christ three times before the cock crew. The Christ foresaw it, and by the simple cock crow, Peter was completely devastated, and brought to tears. That bore a deep mark on Peter's soul. In like manner, we each have such marks that would claim us for Christ's own. The Christ knows our frame.

My embrace of Christianity then, was solely on the strength of Christ Jesus, of His character, of His nature, of who He was in the four gospels, of His deity, His holiness, His righteousness, His absolute Godliness; He was God. It was not a mere intellectual assent; it reached out to the depths of who he was in my limited human understanding. I was emotionally excited and stirred by the depths of his very nature; his truth profoundly moved my heart like a rushing torrent, so intense, like *the wind bloweth where it listeth, and thou hearest the sound thereof, but canst not tell where it cometh, and whither it goeth.*—Luke 3:8. I certainly knew nothing then of the things I know today about the Bible, the Old and New Testaments, of Bible history, doctrines and theology; of conversion, regeneration, salvation, justification, and sanctification. I had only read the four gospels. That only compelled me to follow Christ. He inspired me, convicted me in His way. I have asked for it in a long time, I have sought it in as long a time, and I have knocked at so many wrong doors in so many years of my life, and now I have knocked on the only One Right Door. *Ask, and it shall be given you; seek, and ye shall find; knock, and it shall be opened unto you. For everyone that asketh receiveth; and he that seeketh findeth; and to him that knocketh it shall be opened.*—Matthew 7:7-8.

The four gospels in the Bible was the basis for embracing Jesus Christ. The Bible is the living voice of God; in the beginning was the Word, and the Word was with God and the Word was God. The Word became flesh, and dwelt among us . . . the Word was Jesus. I adored Christ totally; I adored His Word. They are one; they were with each other from the beginning: Christ the Person, His Word the living voice. I loved Him then and He never left me at any time in my life. He is faithful. *I have manifested thy name unto the men which thou gavest me* *out of the world: thine they were, and thou gavest them me; and they have kept thy word.—*John 17:6. *O righteous Father, the world hath not known thee: but I have known thee, and these have known that thou hast sent me. And I have declared unto them thy name, and will declare it: that the love wherewith thou hast loved me may be in them, and I in them.—*John 17:25-26.

The grace of our Lord Jesus Christ is certainly not the fact that He was poor. The grace of our Lord Jesus Christ is this, that though He was rich, for us He became poor. It is this graciousness that has thrilled and awed my heart—not that He whom they worshipped was a servant, but that being in the form of God, He took on Him willingly a servant's form. When the supper ended, He laid aside His garments, and took a towel and washed His disciples' feet. It is a little picture, perfect in its outline, of the life of ministry that was so near its close. And what has awed men in that life of ministry has never been simply its lowliness of toil, but the thought that Christ in bending to His toil had laid aside His garments of eternity. Ye know the grace of the Lord Jesus Christ, that though He was rich, for us He became poor. The conquering wonder of it all is not the poverty; it is the infinite wealth that he gave up for poverty. It is not the manger, it is not the cross; it is the stooping from heaven to the manger and to the cross that has thrilled men as they never could be thrilled by any tale of patient, quiet endurance.

My willingness to read the small edition of the Gideon's Bible (containing the New Testament and Psalms) in the King James Version that begun with the four gospels, truly guided by His gracious hand, borne out of desperation in my search for God and yet not knowing He was the search subject. Left to myself, I would never have picked up that New Testament in my possession for years, to read and re-read. When I surrendered the thought of not reading it in my utter desperation, God graciously drew me unto Him. No amount of resistance would have been possible to keep me away from His call. He chose me; I did not choose Him. Out of His love and mercy, He drew me unto Himself. I did not go to Him. John 15:16 specifically refers to Christ's apostles, but the principle extends to us: "*You did not choose Me, but I chose you and appointed you that you should go and bear fruit, and that your fruit should remain, that whatever you ask the Father in My name He may give you.*" Jesus clearly states in Luke 19: 10, "*For the Son of Man has come to seek and to save that which was lost.*" I was utterly lost yet He was not willing that I should remain lost; He would save me, the lost.

God has not left Himself without a witness in the heart of fallen man. The first man ate of the fruit of the tree of the knowledge of good and evil. God has left in the mind of man the knowledge of right and wrong, in order that he is responsible for his thoughts and deeds, and accountable for all consequences arising from those thoughts and deeds. God has given to every man a conscience; He has not given to every man the Holy Spirit. Man is in his natural element, he is spiritually dead. *They show that the work of the law is written on their hearts, while their conscience also bears witness, and their conflicting thoughts accuse or even excuse them on that day when, according to my gospel, God judges the secrets of men by Christ Jesus.*—Romans 2: 15-16. Until the Holy Spirit is given man still walks in the flesh, he is still the natural man. Jesus had asked God the Father to give us the Holy Spirit. *And I will ask the Father, and he will give you another Helper, to be with you forever, even the Spirit of truth, whom the world cannot receive, because it neither sees him nor knows him. You know him, for he dwells with you and will be in you.*—John 14:16-17. *Those who are in the flesh cannot please God. You, however, are not in the flesh but in the Spirit, if in fact the Spirit of God dwells in you. Anyone who does not have the Spirit of Christ does not belong to him. But if Christ is in you, although the body is dead because of sin, the Spirit is life because of righteousness.*—Romans 8:8-10.

For all the time that I have intentionally and knowingly ignored God, shut Him out of my mind and my heart, avoided Him at all cost, shuttered my eyes to His Word, stopped my ears from His living voice; in His love He worked on me, He bided His time. I ran from Him, I fled from His presence, hid from His truth, mocked His Word, derided His followers, marked an atheist, and a known anti-Christ among friends. In His goodness and mercy, in His abounding Grace He gently tarried, and when I have exhausted all the doors I could knock on, I peeked into His open inviting door . . . His living voice beckoned to my hungering soul. For once, I accepted the invitation, my mind and heart opened, the shutters of my eyes raised, the ear stops came off . . . I went near the living voice, read it, and heard it. All of me saw the light, my soul lifted, He was real; He was alive, He was perfect, He was absolute. *For therein is the righteousness of God revealed from faith to faith: as it is written, "The just shall live by faith." For the wrath of God is revealed from heaven against all ungodliness and unrighteousness of men, who hold the truth in unrighteousness; because that which may be known of God is manifest in them; for God hath shewed it unto them. For the invisible things of him from the creation of the world are clearly seen, being understood by the things that are made, even his eternal power and Godhead so that they are without excuse: because that, when they knew God, they glorified him not as God, neither were thankful; but became vain in their imaginations, and their foolish heart was darkened. Professing themselves to be wise, they became fools, and changed the glory of the uncorruptible God into an image made like to corruptible man, and to birds, and fourfooted beasts, and creeping things. Wherefore God also gave them up to uncleanness through the lusts of their own hearts, to dishonour their own bodies between themselves: who changed the truth of God into a lie, and worshiped and served the creature more than the Creator, who is blessed forever. Amen.—* Romans 1:17-25.

Life after knowing Jesus Christ became 'de-organised' to a new way of thinking and understanding not by force of a mandated structure or system. It was life regenerated from the very premise, the very seat of its existence to its conclusion on this tangible earth, it brought about a change, a transformation from the inside out. As a Buddhist, the author worked and laboured at doing good deeds in order to merit the good outcomes that would benefit his next life through the workings of unexplainable forces of the invisible cause and effect of *karma*. Try hard as he would there was such limitation in man to do well; in himself similarly, the limitation was common and instantly ruled out the very hypothesis in Buddhism as untenable.

Knowing Jesus Christ did not require those deliberate workings and labouring. Good came from the inside out. When you have Christ in you, your mind and heart transform to conform to Christ's nature. Christ transforms us so that we are like Him. *And be not conformed to this world: but be ye transformed by the renewing of your mind, that ye may prove what is that good, and acceptable, and perfect, will of God.*—Romans 12:2. There was absolute liberty. Any goodness we have come from Christ working His nature in us so that we think like Him, we behave like Him, and become like Him. You cannot belabour or summon forth that which you do not possess. Goodness was not a property native to man. Tainted with wickedness, envy, and strife at every act, man harbours an underlying self-centred motive. Every thought veils a self-serving end. There was nothing meritorious that man can bring to the court of God's judgement to present as worthy to appease the wrath of a righteous and holy God. The waywardness of man cannot be excused; his wrongdoing not redeemable by his own reprobate and corrupt nature. Man needs a saviour who can come to God to advocate on his behalf, on the Saviour's own account that has a perpetual eternal credit of acceptance with God such that in the Saviour's name all the evidences for all the wrongs of this world are passed over when placed before the judgement bench.

Endnotes

The verses immediately below, taken from the Old Testament of the Bible speaks of the Lord Jesus Christ. His coming as man was foretold; He fulfilled it in the New Testament. God's spirit rested upon Him that He bore all of God's spirit of wisdom . . . of understanding . . . of counsel . . . of might . . . and of the fear of the LORD.

And there shall come forth a rod out of the stem of Jesse, and a Branch shall grow out of his roots: And the spirit of the LORD shall rest upon him, the spirit of wisdom and understanding, the spirit of counsel and might, the spirit of knowledge and of the fear of the LORD; And shall make him of quick understanding in the fear of the LORD: and he shall not judge after the sight of his eyes, neither reprove after the hearing of his ears: But with righteousness shall he judge the poor, and reprove with equity for the meek of the earth: and he shall smite the earth with the rod of his mouth, and with the breath of his lips shall he slay the wicked. And righteousness shall be the girdle of his loins, and faithfulness the girdle of his reins.—Isaiah 11:1-5.

Thou art fairer than the children of men: grace is poured into thy lips: therefore God hath blessed thee for ever. Gird thy sword upon thy thigh, O most mighty, with thy glory and thy majesty. And in thy majesty ride prosperously because of truth and meekness and righteousness; and thy right hand shall teach thee terrible things. Thine arrows are sharp in the heart of the king's enemies; whereby the people fall under thee. Thy throne, O God, is for ever and ever: the sceptre of thy kingdom is a right sceptre.

Thou lovest righteousness, and hatest wickedness: therefore God, thy God, hath anointed thee with the oil of gladness above thy fellows. All thy garments smell of myrrh, and aloes, and cassia, out of the ivory palaces, whereby they have made thee glad. Kings' daughters were among thy honourable women: upon thy right hand did stand the queen in gold of Ophir. Hearken, O daughter, and consider, and incline thine ear; forget also thine own people, and thy father's house; So shall the king greatly desire thy beauty: for he is thy Lord; and worship thou him. And the daughter of Tyre shall be there with a gift; even the rich among the people shall intreat thy favour. The king's daughter is all glorious within: her clothing is of wrought gold. She shall be brought unto the king in raiment of needlework: the virgins her companions that follow her shall be brought unto thee. With gladness and rejoicing shall they be brought: they shall enter into the king's palace. Instead of thy fathers shall be thy children, whom thou mayest make princes in all the earth. I will make thy name to be remembered in all generations: therefore shall the people praise thee for ever and ever.—Psalms 45:2-17.

Concerning his Son Jesus Christ our Lord, which was made of the seed of David according to the flesh; And declared to be the Son of God with power, according to the spirit of holiness, by the resurrection from the dead:—Romans 1:3-4.

The entire person of Jesus is as one perfect gem, and his life is but one imprint of the seal. He is altogether complete, not only in his several parts, but as a gracious all-glorious whole. His character is not a splash or dabs of fair colours mixed randomly, not a pile of precious stones cast imperfectly or carelessly that lay one upon another; he is a picture of immaculate natural beauty and a breastplate of skilful crafted glory. In him, all the 'things of good repute' are in their proper places, and fitly framed to assist in adorning each other. Not one feature in His glorious person attracts attention at the expense of others; but He is perfectly and altogether lovely.

Jesus tells of power, of grace, of justice, of tenderness, of truth, of majesty, and of timeless immutability that make up such a God-man, as neither heaven nor earth has seen. His infancy, His eternity, His sufferings, His triumphs, His death, and His immortality, all wove in one gorgeous seamless tapestry, without rent. He is music without discord; He is as many, and yet not divided; He is as all things, and yet not diverse. As all the colours blend into one resplendent rainbow, so all the glories of heaven and earth concur in Christ, and unite so wondrously, that there is none like Him in all things; He is the mirror of all perfection.

Whereby are given unto us exceeding great and precious promises: that by these ye might be partakers of the divine nature, having escaped the corruption that is in the world through lust.—2 Peter 1:4.

In the Age of Innocence . . . Out of innocence, we embrace the unknown. Out of ignorance, we fear not the unknown . . . and we freely move forward.

In the Age of Discovery . . . The mirror of discovery reveals the blemishes, the imperfections, the weaknesses, perhaps the difficulties, the uncertainties . . . and we pause to consider the odds.

8.

At Twenty-One—A Brave New World

The lines are fallen unto me in pleasant places;
yea, I have a goodly heritage.
I will bless the LORD, who hath given me counsel:
my reins also instruct me in the night seasons.
I have set the LORD always before me:
because he is at my right hand, I shall not be moved.
—Psalm 16:6-8.

In the age of innocence, we look at things as though all is well even in the surrounding 'unwell'. Not bothered by the adverse, motivations for going forward come from within us. *Out of innocence, we embrace the unknown. Out of ignorance, we fear not the unknown . . . and we freely move forward.*

In the age of discovery, we begin to see all that is unwell and wonder why they are, we are bothered by them and are somewhat held back. One is still learning, discovering, quite uncertain about the hand with

125

which one was dealt; moving forward seems the way to go. *The mirror of discovery reveals the blemishes, the imperfections, perhaps the difficulties, the uncertainties . . . and we pause to consider the odds.*

In the age of restlessness, we see and feel more deeply all that is unwell and want to be involved, to do something to right that which is unwell. Ideas are agitated and brewed to action, yet simmering away below the surface, and remain there as *ideals*. There is a deep and strong desire to change, to break from the status quo.

When moving from innocence to discovery to restlessness: we are like bread firstly unbaked, then partially-baked, and now nearly baked. Perhaps, in the age of brooding to come, as we traverse the elements and circumstance of life we become as baked and ready for meaningful consumption.

As Wordsworth says, *"Whose everlasting purposes embrace all accidents, converting them to good,"* and so our God does not leave anything to chance for all are precious in His eye. Our lives continue in the unexpected but we can be thankful that He does not thrust us into the hands of unknown fate. Our lives are left to a merciful loving heavenly Father who would not let a sparrow fall without Him; who knows the hairs on our heads, every strand that changes in colour, every one that fall out of its place; he tends the common lily in its splendour more breathtaking than all of Solomon's grand palaces. He is ever foreseeing; ever expecting . . . "thou art ever with Me."

A new world is one we always look forward to, where its bountiful benefits and treasured challenges are visibly within reach, from perhaps the promises provided by a quality foundational education, a supportive station in life both in means and standing. A *brave* new world on our own can be fearfully wrought and conceived, without the benefit of foreseeing and knowing what lies in the path ahead:

treachery of the meanest sort or calm weather of the kindliest touch may all be our lot, our portion. Who knows till one arrives. Knowing Christ was of the utmost importance that in one sweep He dealt with and took care of every question, every doubt, every unsolved problem, every condition and place in my life, every question about my beginning and my end, about the way the world was and is and will be. Christ with great craft and wisdom swept away all the misconceived philosophies and arguments concerning Him, and reveal the glorious magnanimity as God yet come as man. By His unquestionable authority, He laid all the noises to noiselessness, all clamouring voices to concord in Him, all doubts in the bed of assurance. All hopes rested in faith in Him alone, in His Word. My affections for Jesus were deeper than those I dare give any other. Pa and Mie could disown me, yet I must follow Christ. I held all earthly glories and traditions with a loose hand, but carried him fast locked in my heart. I voluntarily deny myself for His sake, yet I cannot deny him. It is scant love born of God's election and will, out of the truth that I saw in Jesus and in Him alone. *It is of the LORD'S mercies that we are not consumed, because his compassions fail not. They are new every morning: great is thy faithfulness. The LORD is my portion, saith my soul; therefore will I hope in him. The LORD is good unto them that wait for him, to the soul that seeketh him. It is good that a man should both hope and quietly wait for the salvation of the LORD.—* Lamentations 3:22-23.

Going forth into a brave new world
With Christ our companion;
The fountain of all living waters,
Wherein shall I thirst?
He is ever with us.
He is Immanuel.

Going forth into a brave new world
With Christ our provider;

The source of all provender,
Wherein shall I hunger?
He is ever with us.
He is Immanuel.

Going forth into a rough new world
With Christ our Word;
The source of all wise counsel,
Wherein shall I stray?
He is ever with us.
He is Immanuel.

He is strong. We are weak
He is eternal. We decay and pass on.
He is blameless. We transgress and must repent.
He draws us. We must draw near.
He is ever with us.
He is Immanuel.

So teach us to number our days, that we may apply our hearts unto wisdom. Return, O LORD, how long? and let it repent thee concerning thy servants. O satisfy us early with thy mercy; that we may rejoice and be glad all our days.— Psalm 90:12-14.

Sir Isaac Newton towards the end of his life reminded us in his most inimitable and unforgettable manner: "I have been nothing more than a little child who has picked up a few shells and pebbles on the shore of the ocean of truth."

EPILOGUE

The LORD will perfect that which concerneth me: thy mercy,
O LORD, endureth for ever: forsake not the works of thine own hands.
—Psalm 138:8.

That then the LORD thy God will turn thy captivity,
and have compassion upon thee, and will return and gather thee from all the
nations, whither the LORD thy God hath scattered thee.
—Deuteronomy 30:3.

The Bible in many places portrays God's people as pilgrims on a journey through the wilderness of this life. Our destination, our vision is the Kingdom of God and the path we must tread is often treacherous, trying, and discouraging. His Word, the Bible, is His living voice giving us the inspiration, the guidance in His will, and given to us to deal in the trials and tribulations be they of plenty and want, of joy and suffering, of health and infirmity, of life and death. For in the Bible we see recordings of God's people in the many insurmountable difficulties, impassable obstacles, fiery trials, and overwhelming afflictions; in the Bible we see God's abundant love, bountiful mercies, absolute holiness, and sovereign grace in ordering the times of peace, of wisdom, of plenty. Throughout the Bible man is depicted as inclined to transgress against God's righteousness, thus 'missing the mark', and therefore is separated from His divine and holy nature. Man needs to be reconciled to God and is eternally unable to accomplish this by his very original nature. To bridge this gulf between God and man, God gave us His only Son who is 'one' with Him, to resolve the problem of man's sinful nature once and for all eternity, and restore the blemished relationship with God. *And there shall in no wise enter into it any thing that defileth, neither whatsoever worketh abomination, or maketh a lie: but they which are written in the Lamb's book of life.*—Revelation 21:27

However, we have a constraint in time, *three score and ten years or four score years* to overcome these trials—to ford the slippery streams, cross the overwhelming rivers, trek the treacherous highways, and climb the hazardous mountains—before winter sets in. We have to make every day count to reach the Promised Land that awaits us.

At the end . . . only the eternal matters.

Very often, we hear the wisest and most learned men of science stand ready to admit that what they know is so little, and for all the years they have to live, it would take generations of accumulated and reconstructed knowledge to even understand a speck of the world. They have in every age, expressed their deep humility in their awe of creation, of the workings of science from the smallest particle to the multitude of stars and the expanse and complexity of the universe. The more they know—the more they have confessed the limited extent of their knowledge. Sir Isaac Newton towards the end of his life reminded us in his most inimitable and unforgettable manner: *"I have been nothing more than a little child who has picked up a few shells and pebbles on the shore of the ocean of truth."*

They have all found their rest in the omniscient, omnipotent, and omnipresent God. The vastness of God had confounded them all.

They were humbled . . . by the little they know in the much that they cannot know.

Even the Book of books, our Holy Bible has much in it for the picking, for the learning, for the understanding of the manifold wisdom of our God, our Father. Our Lord Jesus, the Word, is ever the Way, the Truth, and the Life. *"Here am I,"* John Wesley says, *"far from the busy ways of men. I sit down alone, only God is here. In His presence I open, I read His Book, for this end—to find the way to heaven. Does anything appear dark or intricate? I lift my heart to the Father of Lights. I then search after and consider parallel passages of Scripture, comparing spiritual things with spiritual. I meditate thereon with all the attention and earnestness of which my mind is capable. And what I thus learn, that I teach."* For me, what I thus experience and comprehend, that I share till my last breath, be it in writing or speech or walk.

Meeting Jesus was the best thing that ever happened to me. In a moment, the things of yesterday that were in the dark now recast themselves in the light into Christ's mould, His way, and His person. All things became clear. All that one needed to do was to follow Him. Follow Him . . . a seemingly simple command. More awaits in the Age of Brooding when the author discovers that the liberating simple command of FOLLOW ME was such a marvellous call to our willing hearts, and anathema to many else around him as he once was. When obediently willing, the going forth was easy in *spirit*. However, still in our carnal body the *flesh* is weak. The soul buffeted by afflictions arising from conflicts between spirit and flesh, by temptations adamant at slaying the spirit and lifting the flesh. Faith in Christ and His promises is our saving grace . . . . *For ye were sometimes darkness, but now are ye light in the Lord: walk as children of light: (For the fruit of the Spirit is in all goodness and righteousness and truth;) Proving what is acceptable unto the Lord. And have no fellowship with the unfruitful works of darkness, but rather reprove them.*—Ephesians 5:8-11.

Mine eyes shall be upon the faithful of the land, that they may dwell with me: he that walketh in a perfect way, he shall serve me.—Psalm 101:6.

Truly, restlessness dissipated for all the reasons that precipitated it; it was resolved in Christ. My restlessness found no excuse in not having an answer to my beginning and my end, in my existence now and hereafter. It became manifestly clear that I was the root of it all. Completely corrupted in my nature in ignoring God and His Word, I simply refused to acknowledge God as God. I was totally disobedient and wilful. As a hopelessly depraved man, I had no concern for Christ and all the things of God; I was more concerned with my own righteousness in the good works perceived by the world as though they could buy me my future in the here and hereafter through the workings of karma. I laboured and groaned under that yoke of my own virtue and self-righteousness.

In a moment, all that changed when for the first time; in obedience to the prompting of the Spirit, I laid eyes on the Word of God. My soul lighted up, darkness substituted, the burden of disobedience removed, and I saw the Way, the Truth, and the Life in Christ. How could I kick against the pricks for all my life until then? I refused to consider God's grace; I neither hungered nor thirsted for it. It was utter Disobedience. It was sheer Wilfulness. It was simply of a sinful and corrupted nature detestable to a righteous God. A depraved nature has no meekness, has no lowliness in heart, and can find no rest. Christ was obedient unto His Father; we need to learn of Him and take His yoke upon us. In so doing, all became clear as the darkness rolled away, and lightening as the burden lifted. *Come unto me, all ye that labour and are heavy laden, and I will give you rest. Take my yoke upon you, and learn of me; for I am meek and lowly in heart: and ye shall find rest unto your souls. For my yoke is easy, and my burden is light.*—Matthew 11:28-30.

What can I do? I am unable to turn off the truth; I cannot ignore it. The truth is sure and it is firm. Truth is accurate, is precise. It is stable; there is no wavering. It is faithful; it is constant and consistent. All that opposes it is unable to stand in its presence; for they shall melt away under the light of its glorious perfection.

Restlessness had been lived. Will it raise its head again? In the age of brooding, our rest challenged and tested; issues of doubt and of assurance concerning our faith buffet us to rock our balance. We can surely rest in His promise to preserve us in eternity as we continue in faith that He is ever with us.

Restlessness had been lived. Will it raise its head again? In the age of brooding, our rest is challenged, and tested; we may be buffeted with issues of doubt and of assurance concerning our faith. We can surely rest in His promise to preserve us in eternity as we continue in faith that He is ever with us.

A 𝅘𝅥𝅮𝅘𝅥𝅮 TO READERS

You may have read the earlier two books:

- Age of Innocence
- Age of Discovery

This book, **Age of Restlessness** published in soft cover, hard cover, and e-book versions, is available from Trafford Publishing Singapore.

You can also avail of it online at Amazon, Barnes & Noble, Book Depository, Kinokuniya, and many others.

Rejoice with me! We are a book away from completion of the sequel of four books. Watch out for it in October or November 2013.

ACKNOWLEDGEMENTS

My first and highest acknowledgement shall always be to God. I stand wholeheartedly with Andrew Bonar when he wrote, "My righteousness is the righteousness of Him who is God and our Saviour. I see nothing in myself but *that which* would condemn me to eternal banishment from God. I shall be to all eternity a debtor to the Lord my God, never paying one mite, but, on the contrary, hour by hour getting deeper and deeper and deeper in debt to Him who is 'all my salvation and all my desire.' I often exult in the thought that every moment in the ages to come I shall be better and better able to love Him Who loved me from all eternity—Who chose me—Who lived for me that life of obedience, and died that death in order that I, a soul that sinned, might live with Him forever. He rose, ascended, and interceded for me. He presented my name to the Father as one of the lost whom He had found. He is coming in glory soon to claim my body from the grave, and to make me altogether perfect, spotless, glorious, the image of Himself. All to the praise of the glory of His grace! All this is mine because He has enabled me to believe on the beloved Son. 'Accepted in the Beloved' shall be on my forehead along with the Father's name, in New Jerusalem. By grace, through faith: Bless the Lord, O my soul!"

My immediate family, my parents (deceased) and my siblings who may or may not have known about my writing has been a hidden group of silent motivators. Even though 'silent', they have been an ineffaceable part of me as for a purpose.

The many brothers and sisters in my church family who truly have been supportive of my writing endeavour are deserving of my humble thanks from the depths of my heart and soul: a big hearty and deeply grateful embrace to them all. They kindly rendered to me a tender and kindly pulse check of my writing.

The many others in my life who made a cameo appearance in this book or elsewhere in the earlier two books of the 'AGE OF . . .' sequel, as those had not been included in print for want of space and consistency. Life is never an accident and you have all been fitted to His design.

The publishing team at Trafford and their consultants continued to be a blessing.

ABOUT THE AUTHOR

The author is semi-retired, a child of God by divine election, a financial services consultant and writer by calling, a coach by choice, a management consultant by circumstance, and an accountant by training. He is married with two adult children and two grandchildren, and lives in Singapore. He worships at a Bible-believing Baptist church. Robin writes under a pen name.

Robin believes that life is not accidental but has a purposeful design privy only to the Creator. He catches glimpses of it as he reflects on his own life. Time reveals a coherence of all of life's *past* events as he sees them dovetailed or integrated into the ultimate divine purpose.

This book *Age of Restlessness* is the third of a planned sequel that seeks to understand a *concept* of life by reflecting on events and experiences occurring in their chronological stages of development, and revealing the completed part of the divine blueprint as he sees it. The first book was *Age of Innocence* published at the end of 2012. The second, *Age of Discovery* was already out on retail in May 2013. This book, *Age of Restlessness* is the third. A fourth and final book *Age of Brooding*, in the 'Age of . . .' sequel, offers insight into Robin's life between age 22 and

26, before he married and raised a family, should be available at book stores in October/November 2013.

All communications may be directed to the author at his personal email at blessedprobin@gmail.com.

You may visit his facebook page: https://www.facebook.com/pages/Robin-P-Blessed/